BY LAND, SEA, AND SKY

Selected Paganized Prayers and Charms from
Volumes 1 & 2 of the
Carmina Gadelica

By Morgan Daimler

By Land, Sea, and Sky

Copyright 2011 Morgan Daimler

All photography and artwork Copyright 2011 Morgan Daimler

All rights reserved. This book and contents may not be reproduced or transmitted in its entirety by any means, electronic or mechanical, including photocopying, recording, or by any information storage or retrieval systems without permission in writing from Morgan Daimler. Reviewers may quote brief passages.

ISBN 9781791326630

The opinions expressed in this book are solely the opinions of the author. All excerpts and quotes from the Carmina Gadelica are held in the common domain

This book is dedicated to the gods I serve.

To the those who have come before me and those who will follow after.

With thanks to my friends and my family:

To Scott, Amara, Paige.

To Allison, Tricia, Mel, "Herb Lady" Christine, Paige, Chrissy.

To Eilidh, Saille, Moonwriter, Coinneach, Caur, Niall, and my other friends of the OWO

Ní chomain-se th'fhírinne ar thoil daíne

Table of Contents

INTRODUCTION ---1

PART ONE: PRAYER ---3

Chapter 1: Indwelling Prayers ---4
   Imbas with me 2 ---5
   A Prayer 8 ---6
   Desires 19 ---7
   Dedication 42 ---8

Chapter 2: In Praise of the Gods ---9
   Rune of the Muthairn 9 ---10
   Hey the gift, Ho the Gift 59 ---10
   Genealogy of Brighid 70 ---12
   Ocean Blessing 118 ---13
   Prayer: Gods of the Moon 197 ---15

Chapter 3: Blessing and Protection Prayers ---16
   Bless, O gods 10 ---17
   Land, Sea, and Sky 17 ---18
   Guardian Spirit 18 ---19
   Herding Blessing 100 ---20
   Herding Blessing 102 ---21
   Protection 103 ---22
   Prayer for Traveling 116 ---23

Chapter 4: Blessings for Children ---24
   A Bathing Prayer 24 ---25
   Invocation of the graces 3 ---27
   Prayer: Mother's Consecration 200 ---30

Chapter 5: Blessing the Hunt ---31
   Blessing the Hunter 114 ---33
   Consecrating the Chase 115 ---34

Chapter 6: Meal Blessing ---36
   Meal Blessing 78 ---37

Chapter 7: Blessing of the Fire ---40

Blessing of the Kindling 82 ---41
Smooring the Fire 84 ---42

Chapter 8: Sleep Prayers ---44
Sleeping Prayer 29 ---45
Resting Blessing 32 ---45
Sleep Consecration 33 ---46
The Sleep Prayer 35 ---48
Sleep Consecration 36 ---49

Chapter 9: House Protection Prayers ---50
The Soul Shrine 38 ---51
A Resting Prayer 43 ---51
House Protecting 44 ---52
Blessing of the House 45 ---53

Chapter 10: Birth Prayer ---54
Birth Prayer *(page 166)* ---55

Chapter 11: Prayer upon Dying ---56
Soul Peace 53 ---57

Chapter 12: New Moon Prayers ---58
New Moon Prayer 54 ---59
New Moon Prayer (variant) 54 ---60

Chapter 13: Seasonal Prayers ---61
Hogmanay/ New Year's Eve ---62
Hogmanay of the Sack 63 *(unchanged from original)* ---63
Hogmanay Carol 64 ---64
The Song of Hogmanay 65 ---65
Hogmanay 66 ---67
Blessing of the New Year 67 ---68
Imbolc ---69
Imbolc Prayer *(page 169, version 1)* ---71
Imbolc Prayer   *(page 169 version 2)* ---71
Imbolc Prayer *(page 169 version 3)* ---72
Beltane ---72
Beltane Prayer 73 ---73
The Beltane Blessing 74 ---74
The Beltane Blessing 74   *(alternate version)* ---76
Blessing the Seed ---78
Consecration of the Seed 88 ---79
Maunday Thursday ---80
Prayer to the Sea   *(page 163)* ---81

v

June 9th Prayer 69 --81
Reaping Blessings---82
Reaping Blessing 89---83
Reaping Blessing 90---84

PART TWO: MAGIC--85

Chapter 14: Success Charms--86
Justice Charms ---87
Invocation for Justice 20---87
Invocation for Justice 21---88
Victory Charms--89
Prayer for Victory 22 --89
Lustration 23 --90
Lustration – variant 23 --90

Chapter 15: Healing Charms---92
Charms for Mastitis --93
Charm 122--93
Charm 123   (use for humans or livestock) ----------------------------------94
Charm for Dental Issues --95
Charm for a Toothache 126--95
Charms for Sprains and Broken Bones ---96
Charm of the Sprain 130--96
Charm for a Sprain 131 --97
Charm for a Broken Bone 132---97
Charms for Urinary Issues ---98
To Remove Blood from Urine 180---98
A Red Water Charm, for Blood in Urine of Animals 181 ----------------------99
To Remove Kidney Infection with Bleeding 182------------------------------100
Charm for Tumors --100
A Charm to Reduce and Heal Tumors ---------------------------------------101
The Strangles Charm 183 --102
Indigestion Charm 189   (for animals) -------------------------------------103
Indigestion Charm 189   (for people)--------------------------------------104
Swan Lullaby ---106
Lullaby 211 --106

Chapter 16: Protection Charms--111
Consecration of the Cloth 113---112
Fath Fith 133---114
Charms for Lasting Life ---115
Sian a Bheatha Bhuan - A Charm of Lasting Life 134   *Version 1* ------------115
Version 2---117

vi

A Charm Of Lasting Life 135 --- 119
The Spell of the Fox 184 --- 120
The Charm of the Cattlefold 185 --- 120

Chapter 17: Love Charms --- 122
Love Charm 138 --- 123
Love Charm 139 --- 124

Chapter 18: For the Evil Eye --- 126
Exorcism of the Evil Eye 141 --- 127
Counteracting the Evil Eye 142 --- 129
Spell for the Evil Eye 143 --- 131
Charm for the Evil Eye 145 --- 132
A Charm 146 --- 133
Spell Of the Eye 150 --- 134
Spell of the Eye 151 --- 134
Spell for the Eye 152 --- 135
A Charm for Those Who Would Harm Me 193 --- 136

Chapter 19: Herbal and Blessing Charms --- 138
Spell of Counteracting 153 --- 139
The Red Stalk 157 --- 140
The Tree-entwining Ivy 158 --- 141
The Charm of the Figwort 159 --- 142
The Figwort 160 --- 143
The Charm of the Figwort 161 --- 144
The Fairy Wort 162 --- 145
The Yarrow 163 --- 146
The Yarrow 164 --- 147
Saint John's Wort Charm 165 --- 148
St. Columba's Plant Charm 166 --- 148
St. Columba's Plant Charm 167 --- 149
St. John's Wort Charm 168 --- 150
Lucky Shamrock Charm 170 --- 151
Shamrock of Power Charm 171 --- 152
The Mothan Charm 172 --- 153
The Mothan Charm 173 --- 153
The Club Moss 176 --- 155
The Catkin Wool Charm 178 --- 155
Charm of the Churn 191 --- 156
A Charm of Abundance 192 --- 160

Chapter 20: Divination --- 162
Augury Charm 194 --- 163
Omens --- 164

Omen 203 —164
Omen 204 —165
Omen 206 —166
Omen of the Swans 205 —167

CONCLUSION — **168**

APPENDIX A — **171**
A Druid's Baby Blessing Ritual —171

APPENDIX B — **174**
Rites of Passage for Adolscents —174

APPENDIX C — **182**
Imbolc – Traditional Celebrations for a Modern Time —182

APPENDIX D — **187**
Healing Ritual for the Ocean Waters —187

INDEX — **190**

Introduction

These prayers and charms represent a selection of re-paganized versions from Volume 1 and 2 of the Carmina Gadelica as found at http://www.sacred-texts.com/neu/celt/cg1/index.htm The number next to the title of each prayer or charm indicates the reference number of the original within the book, with the charms numbered up to 118 being from the first Volume and the charms numbered above that being from the second Volume. One main difference that readers will note is that the prayers and charms are organized by subject and in some cases the numbering from the original Gadelica will be out of order; however it is believed that this change will make the use of the prayers easier for readers.

The Carmina Gadelica was compiled over a hundred years ago by Alexander Carmichael. Carmichael gathered traditional prayers and charms from the local people in Scotland and organized them into a six volume set of books. The Carmina Gadelica is an essential and vital collection of folk beliefs and practices of the Gaelic Celts. The title – in Latin Carmina Gadelica and in Scots Gaelic Ortha nan Gáidheal – means "songs of the Gael" and these prayers and charms truly represent the songs of the hearts of the people. The original books are well worth studying for anyone interested in learning about the spirituality of the Gaelic peoples. This current work is meant to help further the important cause of establishing modern Celtic polytheistic liturgy based on genuine Celtic sources. I encourage readers to put this book to use and if these versions do not suit you, go to the source and adapt from the originals to your preferences.

This book represents the culmination of two separate projects to paganize the charms and prayers from Volumes 1 and 2 of the Carmina Gadelica. The goal of both the original books was threefold: to paganize the deity references within the prayers, increase accessibility of the spoken charms with modernized language and simultaneously preserve the original spirit and flow of Carmichael's writings. All changes have been kept as minimal as possible and great effort has gone into finding the best, most logical, deity substitutions using the Irish pantheon. The hope driving this project has been that by achieving all three goals these prayers will retain their efficacy, be easier to recite for modern English speakers, and find a place with modern Celtic Polytheists. In short, these prayers and charms are meant to be used.

Morgan Láirbhán, June 1, 2010

Part One: Prayer

Hawthorn leaves emerging in the spring

Chapter 1: Indwelling Prayers

Original pencil drawing by Morgan Daimler

The indwelling prayers are prayers for the inspiration of the Gods and for their presence in a person's life. They can be used both for contemplation, that is recited in a meditative way, and also as an active prayer while making an offering. In many ways they are especially suited for use as morning devotional prayers, but are by no means limited to that.

Indwelling prayers are important because they remind us that the Gods are always with us. Irish mythology is full of examples of deities staying with and helping or hindering people, from Angus mac Og with Diarmuid and Grainne, to the Morrighan and Cu Chulain. These prayers remind us of this connection and help us to consciously strengthen it.

The opening prayer uses the Old Irish word "Imbas" which means inspiration, specifically divine poetic inspiration, and is an important feature of the Druidic practice of filidecht. Filidecht is both sacred poetry and prophecy, and Imbas is something that anyone is able to connect to.

Imbas with me 2

Imbas with me lying down,
Imbas with me rising up,
Imbas with me in each ray of light,
I am a ray of joy with such inspiration,
   I am a ray of joy with such inspiration.

Imbas with me sleeping,
Imbas with me waking,
Imbas with me watching,
Every day and night,
    Each day and night.

Gods with me protecting,
Imbas with me directing,
Imbas with me strengthening,
Forever and for evermore,
    Ever and evermore.

                  ***

A good morning devotional prayer:

A Prayer 8

O Gods,
In my deeds,
In my words,
In my wishes,
In my reason,
And in the fulfilling of my desires,
In my sleep,
In my dreams,
In my repose.
In my thoughts,
In my heart and soul always,
May the blessings of Danu,

And the strength of land, sea, and sky dwell,
>   Oh! In my heart and soul always,
>   May the blessings of Danu,
>   And the strength of land, sea, and sky dwell.

***

Truth is one of the keystones of Druid philosophy as we can see illustrated in these two wisdom sayings called triads, "Three lights that illuminate any darkness: Truth, Nature and Knowledge" and "Three things from which never to be moved: One's oaths, one's gods, and the truth". (Meyer, 1906). This prayer is a good reminder to always walk in truth and seek Truth wherever we go.

Desires 19

May I speak each day according to Truth,
>   Each day may I show your influence O Gods;
>   May I speak each day according to your wisdom,
>   Each day and night may I be at peace.

Each day may I count the numbers of my blessings,
>   May I remember the lessons I have learned;
>   Each day may my heart sing to my Gods,
>   May I sing each day your praises, O Gods.

Each day may my love for you grow stronger,
>   Each night may I do the same;

Each day and night, dark and light,

May I grow stronger in your ways, O Gods.

***

Another good morning devotional prayer:

Dedication 42

Thanks to you, Gods of skill,

Who were with me yesterday

And remain with me today,

Everlasting joy

Is in my soul

With good intent.

And for every gift of peace

You bestow on me.

My thoughts, my words,

My deeds, my desires

I dedicate to You.

I make offerings to You,

As I ask for Your protection,

And Your guidance,

Shield me tonight,

And walk with me each day.

***

Chapter 2: In Praise of the Gods

A picture of a small outdoor altar at the base of an oak tree

These prayers are general invocations and prayers to the Gods which could be used in ritual or in private devotional practice.

Rune of the Muthairn 9

You gods of the moon,
You gods of the sun,
You gods of the planets,
You gods of the stars,
You gods of the earth,
You gods of the sky,
Oh! lovely to look upon,
Are Your shining forms.

Two loops of silk
Down by Your limbs,
Smooth-skinned;
Yellow jewels
And a handful
Out of every stock of them.

Hey the gift, Ho the Gift 59

Hey the Gift, ho the Gift,
   Hey the Gift, on the living.

Gods of the dawn, Gods of the clouds,
Gods of the planet, Gods of the star,

Hey the Gift, ho the Gift,

Hey the Gift, on the living.

Gods of the rain, Gods of the dew,

Gods of the air, Gods of the sky,

Hey the Gift, ho the Gift,

Hey the Gift, on the living.

Gods of the flame, Gods of the light,

Gods of the sphere, Gods of the globe,

Hey the Gift, ho the Gift,

Hey the Gift, on the living.

Gods of the elements, Gods of the powers,

Gods of the moon, Gods of the sun,

Hey the Gift, ho the Gift,

Hey the Gift, on the living.

Gods of skill and much knowledge,

We praise the blessings You grant us,

Hey the Gift, ho the Gift,

Hey the Gift, on the living.

***

The Genealogy of Brighid is one of the better known prayers from the Gadelica, and several versions can be found. In my adaptation I have tried to keep changes minimal, to preserve the flow of Carmichael's version. This prayer is often used by devotees of the goddess Brighid, but may be said by anyone to call on her, for her protection, or for protection on general. It may be said either in the morning, at night, or both. Brighid was one of the pan-Celtic deities known variously as Bríd, Brighid, Brigit, Brigid, Brig, Brigantia, Brigandu, and Bride.

Genealogy of Brighid 70

The genealogy of the holy goddess Brighid,
Radiant flame of gold, noble mother of Ruadan,
Brighid the daughter of an Daghda the Good God,

Brighid daughter of Boann, shining white,
Every day and every night
That I say the genealogy of Brighid,
I shall not be killed, I shall not be harried,
I shall not be jailed , I shall not be wounded,
Nor shall my gods leave me.

No fire, no sun, no moon shall burn me,
No lake, no water, nor sea shall drown me,
No arrow of fairy nor dart of Fay shall wound me,
And I under the protection of the Gods of life,
And my gentle foster-mother is my beloved Brighid

***

This is one of the more interesting prayers in the Gadelica because it involves praying for calm seas at specific points throughout the year. In the original Gadelica version the dates listed are the old pagan fire festivals of Samhain, Imbolc, Beltane, and Lughnasadh as well as the feast days of saints, however each of these feast days is on or within days of a solstice or equinox, so I have shifted the references to these. Taken with a larger view this prayer can be seen as one for peace and safety throughout the year. I would recommend saying it at the turning of the year, but it could be said with equal effectiveness at any point.

Ocean Blessing 118

O gracious gods whom we honor,
Give to us your gracious blessing,
Carry us over the surface of the sea,
Carry us safely to a haven of peace,
Bless our boatmen and our boat,
Bless our anchors and our oars,
Each stay and halyard and traveler,
Our mainsails to our tall masts
May land, sea, and sky remain in their places
That we may return home in peace;
I myself will sit down at the helm,
It is Manannan who will give me guidance,
As He travels far over the waters
On the fields of waves.

On the Autumn Equinox, day of balance,
On Samhain, when the old year ends,

On the day of the Winter Solstice,
Subdue to us the crest of the waves,
On Imbolc, day of my choice,
Cast the serpent into the ocean,
So that the sea may swallow her up;
On the Spring Equinox, day of power,
Reveal to us the storm from the north,
Quell its wrath and blunt its fury,
Lessen its fierceness, kill its cold.

On Beltane Day give us the dew,
On Midsummer's Day the gentle wind,
On Lughnasadh, the great of fame,
Ward off us the storm from the west;
Each day and night, storm and calm,
Be with us, great Gods of Life,
Be our guide in right-living,
Your hands on the helm of our rudder,
By land, sea, and sky

***

This is another great general prayer or invocation. In the fifth line the name of an appropriate goddess should be substituted for the generic "goddess". Lines five and six refer to the ancient practice of the king marrying the goddess of the land to ensure prosperity and luck for the people; however it would be possible depending on the use of the prayer to substitute in an appropriate god name. For example if using this prayer for a Samhain invocation I might choose to use Morrigan for the goddess and an Daghda for the god, in honor of their joining at Samhain in the Irish story of the Cath Maige Tuired. It is left up to the individual to decide what substitutions will work best on each occasion.

Prayer: Gods of the Moon 197

Gods of the moon, Gods of the sun,
Gods of the earth, Gods of the stars,
Gods of the waters, the land, and the skies,
Who walk with us each day.

It was the fair Goddess who blessed the land

It was the divine King who harvested the bounty,
Darkness and tears were set behind,
And the star of guidance went up early.

Brightened the land, brightened the world,
Brightened breeze and current,
Grief was laid down and joy was raised up,
Music was set up with harp and pedal-harp.

Chapter 3: Blessing and Protection Prayers

Original drawing by Morgan Daimler

This first prayer is aimed especially at protection against the world of faery and those creatures within it that might wish us harm.

Bless, O gods 10

Bless, O generous gods,
Myself and everything near me,
Bless me in all my actions,
May I be safe for ever,
    May I be safe for ever.

From every brownie and bansidhe,
From every evil wish and sorrow,
From every nymph and water-wraith,
From every fairy-mouse and grass-mouse,
    From every fairy-mouse and grass-mouse.

From every troll among the hills,
From every siren hard pressing me,
From every ghoul within the glens,
Oh! save me till the end of my days.
    Oh! save me till the end of my days.

***

This short little prayer is an excellent one for daily protection, and might also be used in an emergency situation if the fourth and sixth lines were changed from "with the guiding light of your inspiration" to "under the strong shield of your protection"

Guiding Light of Eternity 11

O gods, who brought me from the rest of last night

To the joyous light of this day,

Bring me through the new light of this day

With the guiding light of your inspiration.

    Oh! through the new light of this day

    With the guiding light of your inspiration.

***

    The Land, Sea, and Sky prayer combines the idea of blessing and protection, calling on several different goddesses for both. I chose the goddesses that made the most sense to substitute in to the original; however the reader should feel free to use whatever combination of three goddesses they feel the most in tune with for this prayer, keeping in mind that care should be given to choose three that are known to have gotten along in mythology and whose energies are not too vastly at odds.

Land, Sea, and Sky 17

Land, sea, and sky be with me

From the top of my face to the edge of my soles.

O Airmed mild, O Danu of glory,

O gentle Brighid of the locks of gold,

Preserve me in my weak body,

The three preserve me on the just path.

    Oh! three preserve me on the just path.

Preserve me as I walk and as I rest,
Preserve me, and I so weak and naked,
Preserve me without offence on the way,
The preservation of the three upon me tonight.
    Oh! The three to shield me tonight.

***

    The prayer to the guardian spirit petitions the person's protective spirit and I do not personally believe that it matters how the person visualizes that spirit. Many cultures have some belief that an individual has supernatural protection, although each culture envisions that protection taking slightly different form. I do not think that it matters whether you believe you are watched over by an animal spirit, a spirit in animal form, a disembodied human spirit, a non-human spirit, or any other type. As long as you have faith that you are protected in some way by a spirit this prayer can be used, preferably on a regular basis, to connect to that spirit and ask for its help watching over you.

Guardian Spirit 18

You guardian spirit who has charge of me
Who watches over me in my coming and going,
You watchful spirit who has charge of me
To make rounds about me this night;

Drive from me every temptation and danger,
Surround me on the sea of unknown peril,

And in the narrows, crooks, and straits,
Keep my coracle, keep it always.

Be a bright flame before me,
Be a guiding star above me,
Be a smooth path below me,
And be a kindly shepherd behind me,
Today, tonight, and for ever.

I am tired and I am stranger,
Lead me through safely;
Until for me it is time to go home
To the place of my kin and my gods.

***

These next three are meant to be said as a protection over herds being sent out to pasture; however each can easily be adapted for use as a protection prayer or charm for any traveler.

This first one would require no change at all to be used by a person or people travelling.

Herding Blessing 100

The keeping of the Gods and the Powers on you,
The keeping of Danu always on you,
The keeping of Lugh and of the Daghda on you,
The keeping of the Morrighan on you going and coming,
And the keeping of Nuada the silver-armed on you,
    King Nuada the silver-armed on you.

The keeping of Brighid the foster-mother on you,
The keeping of Airmed the healing-wise on you,
Of all the Gods of Power and of peace,
Of land, sea, and sky,
And the peace-giving Spirits, everlasting, be yours,
   The peace-giving Spirits, everlasting, be yours

***

     This prayer could stand as it is for use with a traveller or alternately slight changes could be made to the opening lines, and when said by one travelling simply change the pronoun "you" to "I" and "me". For example, for a long car journey the first two lines could be changed to: "Travelling country roads, travelling town roads/ Travelling highways long and wide" and then change "feet" to "wheels". In the same way slight changes could be made to adapt the prayer for any type of travel, as needed.

Herding Blessing 102

Travelling moorland, travelling town land,
Travelling moss land long and wide,
The blessing of the Gods about your feet,
May you return home safe and whole,
   The blessing of the Gods about your feet,
   May you return home safe and whole.

The sanctuary of the Gods of Life
Protecting you going and coming,

And of the strength of your ancestors,

And Brighid of the clustering hair golden brown,

   And of the strength of your ancestors,

   And Brighid of the clustering hair golden brown.

***

      In contrast to the first two, this third prayer would be better said by the one not travelling, when praying for protection on a loved one who is travelling.

Protection 103

Pastures smooth, long, and spreading,

Grassy meadows beneath your feet,

The friendship of the Gods to bring you home

To the field of the fountains,

   Field of the fountains.

Closed be every pit to you,

Smoothed be every knoll to you,

Cozy every exposure to you,

Beside the cold mountains,

   Beside the cold mountains.

The care of Lugh and of Daghda,

The care of Nuada and of Dian Cecht,

The care of Brighid fair and of Danu,

To meet you and to tend you,

Oh! the care of all the band
To protect you and to strengthen you.

***

This prayer has two goals, to make others feel favorable towards the one praying and also to ask for protection from the gods.

Prayer for Traveling 116

Life be in my speech,
Sense in what I say,
The bloom of cherries on my lips,
Till I come back again.

The love the Gods gave
Be filling every heart for me,
The love the Gods gave
Filling me for everyone.

Traversing paths, traversing forests,
Traversing valleys long and wild.
The fair white Danu still uphold me,
The many-skilled Lugh be my shield,
The fair white Danu still uphold me,
The many-skilled Lugh be my shield.

Chapter 4: Blessings for Children

Paige on the day of her Naming ceremony

The following prayer would be said while bathing an infant or young child. Each "handful" would represent a handful of water poured over the child as the line was spoken.

A Bathing Prayer 24

A handful for your age,
    A handful for your growth,
A handful for your throat,
    A flood for your appetite.

For your share of the dainty,
    Crowdie and kale;
For your share of the taking,
    Honey and warm milk.

For your share of the supping,
    Whisked whey and whole milk;
For your share of the spoil,
    With bow and with spear.

For your share of the preparation,
    The yellow eggs of Spring;
For your share of the treat,
    My treasure and my joy,

For your share of the feast
    With gifts and with tribute;
For your share of the treasure,
    Sweetness, my love.

For your share of the chase

    Up the face of the Beinn-a-cheo;

For your share of the hunting

    And the ruling over hosts.

For your share of palaces,

    In the courts of kings;

For your share of victory

    With its goodness and its peace.

The part of you that does not grow at dawn,

    May it grow at twilight;

The part of you that does not grow at night,

    May it grow at the high point of noon.

    The three handfuls

    Of the Secret Three,

    To preserve you

    From every envy,

    Evil eye and death;

    The handful of the Gods of Life,

    The handful of the love of your ancestors,

    The handful of the People of Peace,

        Held by

        Land, sea, and sky.

***

This next prayer is to be said over a young girl as both a blessing and protection. I believe this one would be ideal for a girl transitioning from childhood to young adulthood, around perhaps 12 or 13, or at the onset of menses. It could be worked into a ritual for the girl marking her transition, with a literal washing of her hands and anointing of her head with nine drops of water as the prayer is recited. After reciting the prayer, offerings would be made to the girl's ancestors, the spirits of the land, and the gods. The ritual could be followed by a communal feast (some of which should also be given to the ancestors, daoine sidhe, and gods) and gifts could be given to the girl. While there is no indication that I have seen that such a ritual is historically based, there is no direct evidence contradicting it, and such a ritual done in a modern setting would help reinforce community bonds and establish the girl's place within the group. In some cases such an occasion could mark the beginning of the girl's official training for a role within her Tradition.

Invocation of the graces 3

I wash your palms
In showers of wine,
In the lustral fire,
In the three elements,
In the juice of the rasps,
In the milk of honey,
And I place the nine pure choice graces
In your fair fond face,
    The grace of form,
    The grace of voice,

The grace of fortune,

The grace of goodness,

The grace of wisdom,

The grace of generosity,

The grace of choice honor,

The grace of whole-souled loveliness,

The grace of goodly speech.

Dark is yonder town,

Dark are those therein,

You are the young brown swan,

Going in among them.

Their hearts are under your control,

Their tongues are beneath your foot,

Nor will they ever utter a word

    To give offence to you.

You are shade in the heat,

You are shelter in the cold,

You are eyes to the blind,

You are a staff to the pilgrim,

You are an island at sea,

You are a fortress on land,

You are a well in the desert,

    You are health to the ailing.

Yours is the skill of the Fairy Woman,

Yours is the virtue of Brighid the calm,

Yours is the generosity of Danu, ever-flowing,

Yours is the bounty of Boann the fair,
Yours is the beauty of Aine the lovely,
Yours is the tenderness of Airmed, the gentle,
Yours is the courage of Macha the red,
    Yours is the charm of Fand of the wave.

You are the joy of all joyous things,
You are the light of the beam of the sun,

You are the door of the chief of hospitality,
You are the surpassing star of guidance,
You are the step of the deer of the hill,
You are the step of the steed of the plain,
You are the grace of the swan of swimming,
    You are the loveliness of all lovely desires.

The best hour of the day be yours,
The best day of the week be yours,
The best week of the year be yours,
The best year in the lifetimes of men be yours.

Dagda has come and Ogma has come,
Brighid has come and Aine has come,
Boann and Manannan Mac Lir have come,
Lugh the many skilled has come,
Angus mac Og the beauty of the young has come,
Morrighan of the augury has come,
Dian Cecht, gifted god of healing has come,
And Miach the skilled healer of the host has come,

And Airmed the mild has come,

And the Spirit of true guidance has come,

And Danu, mother of the people of skill has come,

To bestow on you their affection and their love,

To bestow on you their affection and their love.

***

Whispered by a mother into her child's ear when they were leaving the house for a journey.

Prayer: Mother's Consecration 200

May the great Gods be between your two shoulders,

To protect you in your going and in your returning,

May the gods of life be near your heart,

And may they pour blessings upon you--

Oh, may they pour blessings upon you!

***

Chapter 5: Blessing the Hunt

A waterfall at Devil's Hopyard in Connecticut

This prayer was said as a consecration over a hunter before he went out to hunt. A very specific ritual was followed were he was anointed with oil while standing with his feet apart, each foot on a patch of bare ground, then handed a bow (Carmichael, 1900).

Much like the blessing of a king or judge, this blessing came with specific prohibitions that acted as geasa for the hunter throughout his life, usually relating to what animals he could and could not hunt. Specifically nursing or brooding animals were prohibited, as were unweaned or unfledged ones, and resting animals (Carmichael, 1900).

While this prayer could be used for any first time hunter, or for each hunter at the beginning of hunting season each year, it could also be seen as ideal for a modern ritual for boys entering manhood. Much as the earlier prayer for girls that could be modified into a ritual for them this prayer could become the core of an entire ritual marking the boy's transition into young adulthood and their acceptance into the community. If used for this purpose I would suggest that the boys should be around the age of 12 or 13 and that the ritual should be followed by an actual hunt in which the boy participates. Whether or not this is possible, it should follow the same form as the one for girls and include a feast for the child afterwards.

Blessing the Hunter 114

You are the product of your ancestors,

May you be guided in the way that is right,

In the names of the Spirits of land, sea, and sky,

In names of the Gods of Life who bless you.

In the names of Ogma, and Nuada

Manannan of the wave, and Daghda the Good God,

Dian Cecht the healer, and Giobnui the smith

Macha the red, and Danu the mother of the aos sidhe.

In the name of Lugh the many-skilled,

And Boann of the river,

Angus beloved, and sovereign Eriu,

Tailtiu calm, and Brighid of the milk and cattle.

In the name of Morrighan goddess of hosts,

In the name of Anu, giver of abundance,

In the name of Flidias of the woodland glens,

And Airmed of the healing herbs.

The time you shall have closed your eyes,

You shall not bend your knee nor move,

You shall not wound the duck that is swimming,

Never shall you harry her or her young.

The white swan of the sweet gurgle,

The speckled dun of the brown tuft,

You shall not cut a feather from their backs,
Till the world ends, on the crest of the wave.

They must be on the wing
Before you place missile to your ear,
And the fair Danu will give you of her love,
And the lovely Brighid will give you of her blessing.

You shall not eat fallen fish nor fallen flesh,
Nor one bird that your hand shall not bring down,
Be thankful for the one,
Though nine should be swimming.

The fairy swan of Brighid of flocks,
The fairy duck of Danu of the people of peace.

***

This next one is to be said by a hunter as he heads out in the morning. When he comes across the first three-way stream he should bend down and wash his face in its water while saying the prayer.

Consecrating the Chase 115

By land, sea, and sky,
In word, in deed, and in thought,
I am bathing my own hands,
In the light and in the elements of the sky.

Vowing that I shall never return in my life,
Without fishing, without fowling either,
Without game, without venison down from the hill,
Without fat, without blubber from out the copse.

O Danu tender-fair, gentle-fair, loving-fair,
Let me avoid the silvery salmon dead on the salt sea,
A duck with her brood an it please you to show me,
A nest by the edge of the water where it does not dry.

The grey-hen on the crown of the knoll,
The black-cock of the hoarse croon,
After the strength of the sun has gone down,
May you let me avoid the hearing of them.

O Danu, mighty mother of the aos sidhe,
Crown me with the crown of your peace,
Place your own regal robe of gold to protect me,
And bless me with success on my hunt today,
    Bless me with success on my hunt today.

***

Chapter 6: Meal Blessing

Hawthorne berries in the fall

This is a longer prayer to be said over food. I would suggest saying it either while cooking or while serving the meal, as opposed to after serving it. Interestingly the prayer contains a line referencing asperging those about to eat after they sit at the table, especially the children. There is a reference as well to several herbs, which might be seen as bringing blessing or luck based on the context; it would be worth considering placing a tiny amount of each, or several, into water to use for sprinkling on the family and guests. I would not recommend drinking or otherwise consuming the water or herbs without carefully researching each for safety, but external application should be all right. Someone seeking to reconstruct a meal practice might work out a system, particularly for ritual meals or feasts, of saying this blessing over the food, serving the meal and then asperging the gathered people with blessed herbal water before the meal commences.

Meal Blessing 78

Every meal beneath my roof,
They will all be mixed together,
In name of the Gods,
    Who gave them growth.

Milk, and eggs, and butter,
The good produce of our own flock,
There shall be no dearth in our land,
    Nor in our dwelling.

In name of the Gods of life,

Who bequeathed to us the power,

With the blessing of the land,

    And of the goddess of the land.

May we appreciate what we have,

And may You be a sanctuary around us,

Ward from us spectre, sprite, oppression,

    And preserve us.

Consecrate the produce of our land,

Bestow prosperity and peace,

In name of Danu the Mother of the aos sidhe,

    And of the three gods of skill.

Dandelion, smooth garlic,

Foxglove, woad, and butterwort,

The three carle-doddies,

    And marigold.

Gray 'cailpeach' plucked,

The seven-pronged seven times,

The mountain yew, ruddy heath,

    And madder.

I will put water on them all,

In the name of Lugh of the Long Arm,

In the name of Daghda the generous,

    And of Macha, sovereign queen.

When we shall sit down

To take our food,

I will sprinkle in the name of the Gods

    On the children.

Chapter 7: Blessing of the Fire

Blessing a fire was an important aspect of starting each day. Fire was seen as a gift from the gods which gave warmth, cooked food, and reminded us always that we also need constant renewal (Carmichael, 1900).

This first prayer would be ideal for use as a morning devotional if combined with the act of lighting a candle. Even if an actual flame is not possible it might be useful to say this prayer and meditate on what it says and on the concepts of the spiritual flame that burns within all of us and must be nourished.

Blessing of the Kindling 82

I will kindle my fire this morning
In presence of the spirits of my hearth,
In presence of the aos sidhe of the loveliest form,
In presence of the gods of life,
Without malice, without jealousy, without envy,
Without fear, without terror of any one under the sun,
But the strength of the Gods to shield me.
> Without malice, without jealousy, without envy,
> Without fear, without terror of any one under the sun,
> But the strength of the Gods to shield me.

Gods, kindle within my heart
A flame of love to my neighbor,
To my family, to my friend, to my kindred all,
To the brave, to the wise, to the servant,
O Gods of might and power,

From the lowliest thing that lives,
To the highest of all.
   O Gods of might and power,
   From the lowliest thing that lives,
   To the highest of all.

***

     This is a prayer to be said when smooring a fire before bed at night, as such it could be used by anyone who uses a woodstove or fireplace for heat overnight. The wording of this one would also serve well as general night prayer to call protection on a home. For those without any nightly fires to be smoored, perhaps this prayer could be recited during a brief period of meditation and reflection over the day's events. Alternately a person could stand in a significant place in their home – by their altar, by the hearth or by the front door – and recite the prayer.

Smooring the Fire 84

The strength of the Gods
To save,
To shield,
To surround
The hearth,
The house,
The household,
This eve,

This night,

Oh! this eve,

This night,

And every night,

Each single night.

Chapter 8: Sleep Prayers

Paige and Binx sleeping

These prayers are to be said just before going to sleep, to call for protection and blessing upon the body throughout the night and the soul during whatever nocturnal journeys it might make.

The first two prayers call on three different types of spirits: the gods, beneficial Otherworldly spirits, and the person's ancestors.

Sleeping Prayer 29

I am placing my soul and my body

Under your protection this night, O Gods,

Under your protection, O mighty ancestors,

Under your protection, O goodly-inclined spirits,

    The Three who would defend my cause,

    May they not turn Their backs upon me.

Gods, who are kind and just,

Ancestors, whose souls live still,

 Spirits of strength and power,

Keep me this night from harm;

    The Three who would protect me

    Keep me this night and always.

***

Resting Blessing 32

In the names of the Holy Powers,

And of the Spirits of the land,

In name of those who have come before me,

    I lay down to rest.

If there is any evil threat or danger,

Or covert act being aimed at me,

Gods free me from it and encompass me,

    And drive from me my enemy.

In name of the Holy Powers,

And of the Spirit of the land,

In name of those who have come before me,

    I lay down to rest.

Gods, help me and encompass me,

    From this hour till the hour of my death.

***

    This prayer calls on various deities in specific, and the gods in general, to guard over the sleeper and to protect them while they are helpless.

Sleep Consecration 33

I lie down tonight

Under the eyes of fair Danu and her sons,

Under the cloak of the Morrigan's protection,

And with Brighid beneath her mantle.

I lie down with the Gods,

May the Gods remain with me,

I will not lie down with opposing forces,

Nor will opposing forces remain with me.

O Gods of the Otherworld,

Help me this night,

Grant me your protection

And the strength of your shields.

You Gods of truth,

Do not forget me in your halls,

Do not turn from me in my need,

Do not exclude me from your people.

    O, you mighty gods of truth

Do not exclude me from your people.

***

    Sleep Prayer # 35 asks for protection on a person's soul as it travels through the night. It also asks that the soul be reunited with the body to see the light of another day, or else – should the person die in the night – that their soul may remain with the gods they love and rejoin their ancestors who have gone before. In many Celtic myths the land of the dead and the land of the gods are either one and the same or are not distinctly separate realms, so there is no contradiction in asking to be remain both with the gods and with the ancestors.

The Sleep Prayer 35

I am going to sleep,

May I wake in health;

If this should be my death-sleep,

With the company of my ancestors,

O Gods of Goodness, may I in peace awake;

    With the company of my ancestors,

    O Gods of Goodness, may I in peace awake.

May my soul remain near to you, O Gods,

Rulers of the three realms;

It was you who have walked with me,

Through the journey of my life,

    Encompass me this night, O Gods,

    That no harm, no evil shall befall me.

While my body is dwelling in sleep,

My soul is soaring in the shadow of the Otherworld,

May goodly spirits ever stay with my soul,

    Early and late, night and day,

    Early and late, night and day.

***

    Sleep Prayer #36 is very similar to #35, with only a slight variance at the end, where the person asks to be kept from sadness and sorrow in life.

Sleep Consecration 36

I am lying down tonight,

With my beloved dead, with the Gods of Power,

With the Spirits of strength and truth,

Who shield me from harm.

I will not lie with evil,

Nor shall evil lie with me,

But I will lie down with the Gods,

And the Gods will protect me.

Gods and ancestors and Spirits,

By the power of land, sea, and sky,

Protect me as I sleep and as I wake,

From the top of my head to the soles of my feet.

Gods of the sun and of the stars,

Gods of skill and of power,

Keep me from the glen of tears,

And from the house of grief and gloom,

    Keep me from the glen of tears,

    From the house of grief and gloom.

Chapter 9: House Protection Prayers

A Ladybug on a Hawthorne leaf

This prayer is said as the last family member goes to bed, to bless and protect the home (Carmichael, 1900). This is a dual purpose prayer, asking both for protection on the home and family and blessing of the same.

The Soul Shrine 38

Gods of Skill, give charge to the spirits,
    To keep guard around my home tonight,
A band sacred, strong, and steadfast,
    That will shield this soul-shrine from harm.

Safeguard , O Gods, this household tonight,
    Ourselves and our means and our fame,
Keep us from death, from distress, from harm,
    From the fruits of envy and of enmity.

Give to us, O Gods of peace,
    Thankfulness for the blessings we have,
A desire to seek and follow the Truth,
    And to give honor to the old ways.

This is a wonderful all-purpose prayer for protection on the home and all within it. It is intended to be said at night; however it could easily be adapted for use whenever a person feels their home is threatened by changing the words "tonight" and "night" to other appropriate time markers.

A Resting Prayer 43

Gods shield the house, the fire, the animals,
Everyone who dwells here tonight.

Shield myself and my beloved group,
Preserve us from violence and from harm;
Preserve us from foes this night,
For the sake of the dedication I owe to you,
In this place, and in every place where your children dwell tonight,
On this night and on every night,
    This night and every night.

***

Here is another good general house blessing prayer. For people without livestock simply remove the lines referring to them.

House Protecting 44

O Gods, bless the world and all that is therein.
Gods, bless my spouse and my children,
Gods, bless the eye that is in my head,
And bless, O Gods, the handling of my hand;
What time I rise in the morning early,
What time I lie down late in bed,
    Bless my rising in the morning early,
    And my lying down late in bed.

Gods, protect the house, and the household,
Gods, consecrate the children and the mothers,
Gods, encompass the flocks and the young;
Be after them and tending them,

What time the flocks ascend hill and wood,
What time I lie down to sleep,
    What time the flocks ascend hill and wood,
    What time I lie down in peace to sleep.

***

Blessing of the House #45 is another highly versatile prayer. It can be used at any point to bless a home, but would lend itself well to the ritual blessing of a new home when a person or family first moves in, or to complete a ritual cleansing of a home.

Blessing of the House 45

Gods bless this house,
From site to stay,
From beam to wall,
From end to end,
From ridge to basement,
From balk to roof-tree,
From foundation to summit,
    Foundation and summit.

***

Chapter 10: Birth Prayer

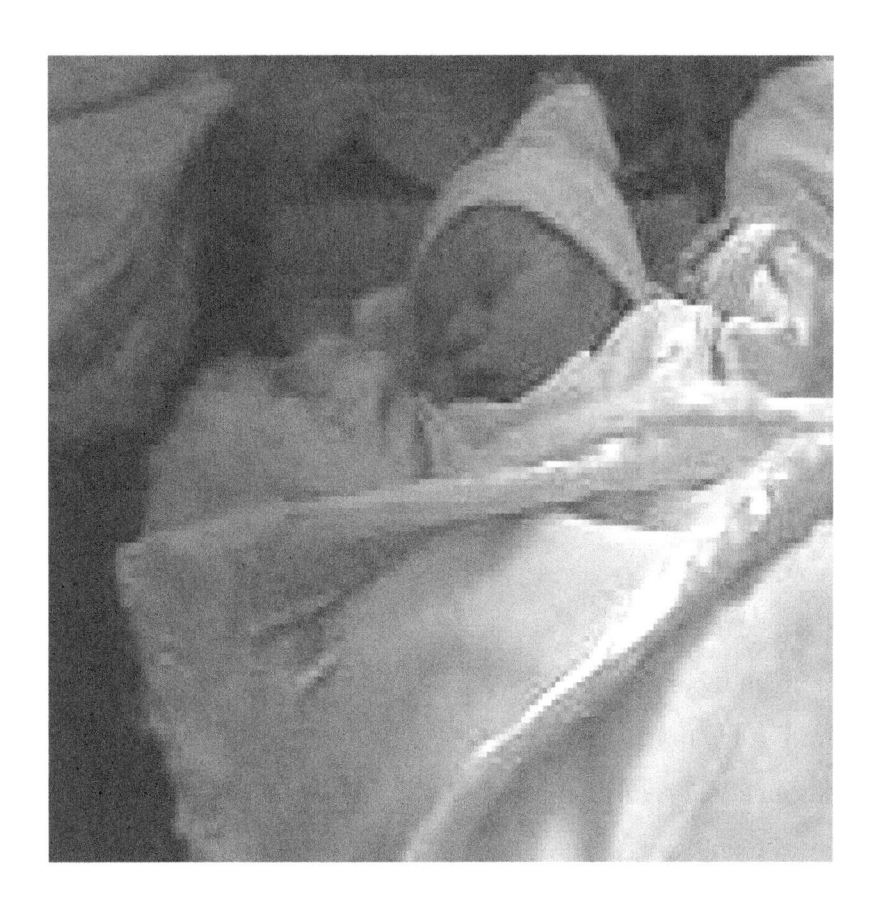

Paige, two days old

The following prayer was said by the midwife or her assistant when a woman was in labor. The woman saying the prayer would stand in the doorway, holding the door frame on either side and recite the following prayer (Carmichael, 1900). There is clearly an important connection between the person standing in a liminal space to say the prayer and the liminal nature of birth itself. Volume 3 of the Gadelica has several beautiful baby blessing rituals in it that I highly recommend.

<u>Birth Prayer</u>   *(page 166)*
Brighid! Brighid! Come in,
Your welcome is truly made,
Give relief to this woman,
And give the conception to the Gods of life.

***

Chapter 11: Prayer upon Dying

Winter berries covered in ice after a storm

This is a blessing to be said at death. This could work equally well as something said to a dying person as they pass or as something said to those who are grieving during a funeral or memorial service.

Soul Peace 53

Since we know the soul is immortal ---
At the time of yielding the life,
At the time of pouring the sweat,
At the time of offering the life,
At the time of shedding the blood,
At the time of balancing the beam,
At the time of severing the breath,
At the time of loosing the soul,
Peace upon the soul's journey;
As it returns to the land from whence it came,
Peace upon the soul's journey,
   As it returns from whence it came.

And may Manannan, gentle and kindly,
Lord of the waves and guide across worlds,
Take possession of the beloved soul,
And shield it home,
   Oh! Where it may rest and be reborn again.

***

Chapter 12: New Moon Prayers

The crescent moon

These payers are said upon seeing the first sliver of the new moon in the sky. They are usually accompanied by a physical action, in some cases turning the coins in your pocket or the rings on your finger, or else bowing or nodding in the direction of the moon (Carmichael, 1900).

There is occasionally some confusion about what is meant by the term "new moon" as opposed to "dark moon". The new moon traditionally was the first sliver of moon that could be seen in the night sky after the dark moon. The dark moon was the period of about three days when the moon was absent from the night sky.

The following prayers were to be said upon the first sighting of the new moon in the sky, and the words would be accompanied by one of the suggested actions. Personally I have always bowed my head slightly to the new moon and kissed my closed fist in a salute, but I do not remember where I learned to do this. The goal of these prayers is similar to that of a charm, and indeed they could be seen as a simple sort of charm, with the recitation of the prayer and the accompanying action being done to draw luck and money to the person.

New Moon Prayer 54

In the name of Danu, mother of the People of Skill,
In the name of the Daghda, Good God of great Skill,
In the name of Lugh, master of many skills,
Oh! In name of the Three who shield us in every need,

If you have found us well tonight,

Seven times better may you leave us without harm,

    You bright white Moon of the seasons,

    Bright white Moon of the seasons.

New Moon Prayer (variant) 54

May your laving luster leave us

    Seven times still more blessed.

O moon so fair,

May it be so,

As seasons come,

And seasons go.

                      ***

Chapter 13: Seasonal Prayers

A Hawthorne tree in flower, one traditional sign of the proper time to celebrate Beltane in the spring.

Hogmanay/ New Year's Eve

To quote the Carmina Gadelica page 149 *"The 'gillean Callaig' carolers or Hogmanay lads perambulate the townland at night. One man is enveloped in the hard hide of a bull with the horns and hoofs still attached. When the men come to a house they ascend the wall and run round sunwise, the man in the hide shaking the horns and hoofs, and the other men striking the hard hide with sticks. The appearance of the man in the hide is gruesome, while the din made is terrific. Having descended and recited their runes at the door, the Hogmanay men are admitted and treated to the best in the house. The performance seems to be symbolic, but of what it is not easy to say, unless of laying an evil spirit. That the rite is heathen and ancient is evident."*

The pagan elements of this practice are evident, including the use of the bull hide and the ritual circling of the house three times sunwise. I believe this may have been done to both drive away any negative spirits as well as to call a blessing on the home in anticipation of the New Year. I believe these prayers could work equally well at the time of secular New Year or at whatever date for the New Year (such as Samhain) a Tradition might choose to celebrate. The prayers focus not on calendar dates so much as the shift in energy surrounding a changing year. I personally think that it is possible that these prayers were originally associated with Samhain, since they involve customs we know to be connected to that holiday, such as dressing in costume and going from house to house requesting food; however those facts alone are not conclusive as other pagan holidays also feature these practices. It does support the idea of shifting the use of these prayers to Samhain for people or Traditions that choose to celebrate only the four Celtic fire festivals, although they would of course be equally valid at the winter solstice for those who choose to celebrate then.

This first prayer is a song or chant sung by the guisers who went door to door.

Hogmanay of the Sack 63 *(unchanged from original)*

Hogmanay of the sack,
Hogmanay of the sack,
    Strike the hide,
    Strike the hide.
Hogmanay of the sack,
Hogmanay of the sack,
    Beat the skin,
    Beat the skin.
Hogmanay of the sack,
Hogmanay of the sack,
    Down with it! up with it!
    Strike the hide.
Hogmanay of the sack,
Hogmanay of the sack,
    Down with it! up with it!
    Beat the skin.

Hogmanay of the sack,

Hogmanay of the sack.

***

These next two were also sung by the guisers travelling from house to house. These songs could be used in a modern setting by anyone re-enacting this folk practice, or could be used as a part in a ritual to symbolically represent the servant of the gods who travelled and blessed the generous households who offered them food.

Hogmanay Carol 64

I have come now to your country,

To renew to you the Hogmanay,

I need not tell you of it,

It was in the time of our ancestors.

I ascend by the door lintel,

I descend by the doorstep,

I will sing my song becomingly,

Mannerly, slowly, mindfully.

The Hogmanay skin is in my pocket,

Great will be the smoke from it presently.

The man of the house will get it in his hand,

He will place its nose in the fire;

He will go sunwards round the children,

And seven times around the housewife.

The housewife it is she who deserves it,

The hand to dispense to us the Hogmanay,

A small gift of the bloom of summer,

Much I wish it with the bread.

Give it to us if it is possible,

If you may not, do not detain us;

I am the servant of the Gods at the door,

Arise and open to me.

***

The Song of Hogmanay 65

Now since we came to the country

To renew to you the Hogmanay,

Time will not allow us to explain,

    It has been so since the age of our fathers.

Ascending the wall of the house,

Descending at the door,

My carol to say modestly,

    As becomes me at the Hogmanay.

The Hogmanay skin is in my pocket,

Great the smoke that will come from that;

No one who shall inhale its odor,

    Shall fail to be healthy from it.

The man of the house will get it in his grasp,

He will put its point in the fire;

He will go sunwise round the children,

    And very specially round his wife.

The wife will get it, it is she who deserves it,

The hand to distribute the Hogmanay,

The hand to bestow upon us cheese and butter,

    The hand without stinginess, without meanness.

Since drought has come upon the land,

We do not expect any delicacy,

A little of the substance of the summer,

    Would we desire with the bread.

If we are not to have it,

If you may, do not detain us;

I am the servant of the Gods on Hogmanay,

    Arise and open the door.

    Hogmanay here! Hogmanay here!

***

    This next one is similar to the previous two, but differs in that it came with specific instructions for the actions of the guisers. After the first verse, if the guisers have been greeted well and rewarded with food they will go three times sunwise around the fire singing a blessing on the house. But if they are not greeted well and rewarded there are specific instructions given for cursing the home which involve walking counter-clockwise around the fire three times and then walking out of the house and raising a stone cairn by the door, before chanting a curse upon the household that calls upon several different types of animals and the negative spirits of the world. This is fascinating as an example of a curse within the Carmina Gadelica that involves clear and specific actions and the creation of a physical item, in this case the cairn. This reminds me of the modern American practices of trick-or-treating related to Halloween where the costumed revelers offer the home owner a choice of giving them a treat or being tricked.

***

Hogmanay 66

(The guisers come singing to the door)

We have come to the door,
To see if we will be the better for our visit,
To tell the generous women of the house
That tomorrow is New Year's Day.

(If the guisers are well treated and rewarded then they proceed three times sunwise around the house's fire singing)

May the Gods bless the dwelling,
Each stone, and beam, and stave,
All food, and drink, and clothing,
May health always be found here.

(If the guisers are not well treated they walk round the fire "withershins" and walk out, raising a cairn in or near the door, called 'carnan mollachd,' cairn of malison. They stomp loudly

and shake the dust off their shoes while intoning the following curse)

The malison of the Gods and of Hogmanay be on you,
And the curse of the plaintive buzzard,
Of the hen-harrier, of the raven, of the eagle,
And the curse of the sneaking fox.

The curse of the dog and of the cat be on you,
Of the boar, of the badger, and of the wild pig,
Of the hipped bear and of the wild wolf,
And the curse of the foul Fomorians.

***

This prayer is commonly said first thing in the morning of the first day of the new year (Carmichael, 1900).

This prayer is meant to be said on the first day of the New Year, whenever you believe that is. It is a request for a fresh start in a fresh year and blessings on the person, their family, and home.

Blessing of the New Year 67

Gods, bless to me this new day,
Never vouchsafed to me before;
As I bless you on this morning,
Embracing the time I am given.

Bless my two eyes,
May my eyes bless all I see;

I will bless my neighbor,

May my neighbor bless me.

Gods, give me a clean start,

Let me remain under your protection;

Bless my children and my wife (husband),

And bless my means and my cattle.

(Alternate final line: And bless my life and my possessions.)

***

Imbolc

Imbolc is a holy day dedicated to the Goddess Brighid and celebrated on February 1st or 2nd, although Carmichael mentions an older date as well of February 13th. The Gadelica mentions several traditions relating to this holiday.

In Scotland the practice is to shape a corn sheaf into a doll, dressing it up and decorating it with pretty shells and stones as well as any flowers that can be found. Girls dressed in white and with their hair down process to each house singing songs to Brighid. At each home the people pay homage to the Goddess figure and offer it gifts of the same type that it is decorated with, except for mothers who offer it little cakes, cheeses or some butter. When finished the girls retire to a house and make a feast for Brighid, where all the boys must petition entrance to honor Brighid. A festive party is then held with music and dancing until dawn. Afterwards the leftovers are distributed to the poor of the community (Carmichael, 1900).

In Ireland it is the butter churn which is dressed as the Brighid doll. After dressing it the girls all dress in their best and bring offerings to the doll along the same lines as those in Scotland. In addition a Brighid's cross is pinned to the dolls chest (Carmichael, 1900).

Another practice on Imbolc Eve is to weave a small bed and then fashion a doll out of oats or corn, which is then dressed and decorated with as much care as if it were a living child. When this bed is ready the woman of the house goes to the door and with her hands on the doorjamb to each side, speaks out to the darkness, announcing that Brighid's bed is ready. Another woman standing behind her asks to invite Brighid in and the first woman announces again that the bed is ready and invites Brighid in to bless the house. The doll is placed with great ceremony in the bed and next to it is laid a birch, broom, bramble or willow wand with the bark removed to signify purity and Truth. It is said that such a wand was given to the High Kings of Ireland and that it must be straight to signify justice and white wood to signify purity and lack of bloodshed. The ashes of the fire are carefully smoothed and in the morning are checked for any sign of disturbance; should the marks of the wand be found it is a blessing on the house, but the greatest blessing is the sign of a footprint in the ashes. These marks indicate Brighid's presence and blessing upon the home. Should the ashes be undisturbed it is believed that Brighid has passed the house over and this is seen as an ill omen. To regain her favor the family burns incense on the hearth and buries alive a chicken where three streams meet. (Carmichael, 1900).

Dandelions are associated with Brighid as are the birds the Linnet and Oystercatcher. Another tradition was connected to the belief that it was on Imbolc that the snakes re-emerged and several prayers relate to this (Carmichael, 1900).

Imbolc Prayer *(page 169, version 1)*

Early on Brighid's morn
The serpent shall come from the hole,
I will not molest the serpent,
Nor will the serpent molest me.

***

Imbolc Prayer   (page 169 version 2)

The Feast Day of the Brighid,
The serpent shall come from the knoll,
I will not touch the serpent,
Nor shall she harm me.

On the Feast Day of Brighid,
The head will come off the 'caiteanach,'
The serpent will come from the knoll
With tuneful whistling.

The serpent will come from the hole
   On the brown Day of Brighid,

Though there should be three feet of snow
   On the flat surface of the ground.

***

Imbolc Prayer *(page 169 version 3)*

On the day of Brighid of the white hills
The noble queen will come from the knoll,
I will not molest the noble queen,
Nor will the noble queen molest me.

***

Beltane

   Beltane is celebrated on the first day of May, when all the fires are extinguished. A need-fire is made at a high place, like a hill top, and then divided into two and all the local livestock are driven between the two fires for blessings. Afterwards each person takes home a bit of the need-fire to re-light their own home fire. (Carmichael, 1900).

   The exact dating of Beltane varies slightly but is generally given in early May; I encourage readers who do not already have a set date to celebrate to research independently and decide what dating fits them and their geographical area the best. Alexei Kondrateiv's book <u>The Apple Branch</u> and Ellen Evert Hopman's book <u>A Druid's Herbal for the Sacred Earth Year</u> are both excellent places to start.

The following prayer would be useful either as a solitary prayer on Beltane morning or as a ritual piece. If said as a solitary prayer I would recommend reciting it either before your altar or standing outside if you own or rent land.

Beltane Prayer 73

Bless, O Gods of life and power,

Myself, my spouse, and my children,

My tender children and their beloved mother at their head.

On the fragrant plain, on the high mountain,

   On the fragrant plain, on the high mountain.

Everything within my dwelling or in my possession,

All cattle and crops, all flocks and corn,

From Samhain Eve to Beltane Eve,

With good progress and gentle blessing,

From sea to sea, and every river mouth,

   From wave to wave, and base of waterfall.

May all that I have be under the guard of the Old Gods,

May they protect me in truth;

Oh! satisfy my soul as I journey through this year,

And shield my loved ones beneath your powerful hands,

   Shield my loved ones beneath your powerful hands.

Bless everything and every one,

Of this little household by my side;

Place the shield of Lugh on us with the power of love,
Till we leave this mortal life behind,
    Till we leave this mortal life behind,

What time the cattle shall forsake the stalls,
What time the sheep shall forsake the folds,
What time the goats shall ascend to the mount of mist,
May the tending of the Spirits follow them,
    May the tending of the Spirits follow them.

You Beings who have been with me since the beginning,
Listen and attend me as I honor you now,
Morning and evening as is becoming in me,
In your presence, O Gods of life,
    In your presence, O Gods of life.

***

This next prayer would have the same uses as the previous but has a stronger agricultural feel. For those that do not own livestock I might suggest changing the pertinent lines, so I will offer an urban alternative following this one.

The Beltane Blessing 74

Danu, mother of the people of skill,
Bless our flocks and bearing cattle;
Do not let hate and curses come near us,
Drive from us the ways of the wicked.

Keep your eyes every Monday and Tuesday
On the bearing cattle and the pairing goats;
Accompany us from hill to sea,
Gather thyself the sheep and their progeny.

Every Wednesday and Thursday be with them,
Your gracious hands always about them;
Tend the cows down to their stalls,
Tend the sheep down to their folds!

Every Friday be at their head,
Lead the sheep from the face of the bens,
With their innocent little lambs following them,
Encompass them with your encompassing.

Every Saturday be likewise with them,
Bring the goats in with their young,
Every kid and goat to the sea side,
And from the Rock of Aegir on high,
With tresses green about its summit.

The strength of the Morrighan be our shield in distress,
The strength of Brighid, her peace and her passion,
The strength of Airmed, gentle healer,
And of the Good God, Daghda, wisest of all.

And of every other God in kinship with them
And who is one of the people of Danu.

Bless ourselves and our children,

Bless every one who shall come from our loins,

Bless him whose name we bear,

Bless, O Gods her from whose womb we came.

Every holiness, blessing and power,

Be yielded to us every time and every hour,

In name of the Gods of life,

By land, sea, and sky.

Be the blessing of Morrighan to shield us downward,

Be the blessing of Morrighan to shield us upward,

Be the blessing of Morrighan to shield us roundward,

Accepting our Beltane blessing from us,

    Accepting our Beltane blessing from us.

                      ***

The Beltane Blessing 74   *(alternate version)*

Danu, mother of the people of skill,

Bless our home and all within;

Do not let hate and curses come near us,

Drive from us the ways of the wicked.

Keep your eyes every Monday and Tuesday

On our house and possessions and lives;

Accompany us from hill to sea,

Gather us in under your golden cloak.

Every Wednesday and Thursday be with us,

Your gracious hands always about us;

Watch over us as we work,

Watch over us as we rest!

Every Friday be at our head,

Lead us away from any danger,

And protect our helpless little children from harm,

Encompass us with your encompassing.

Every Saturday be likewise with us,

Bring to us luck and prosperity,

As we travel to the sea side,

And from the Rock of Aegir on high,

With tresses green about its summit.

The strength of Morrighan be our shield in distress,

The strength of Brighid, her peace and her passion,

The strength of Airmed, gentle healer,

And of the Good God, Daghda, wisest of all.

And of every other God in kinship with them

And who is one of the people of Danu.

Bless ourselves and our children,

Bless every one who shall come from our loins,

Bless him whose name we bear,

Bless, O Gods her from whose womb we came.

Every holiness, blessing and power,
Be yielded to us every time and every hour,
In name of the Gods of life,
By land, sea, and sky.

Be the blessing of Morrighan to shield us downward,
Be the blessing of Morrighan to shield us upward,
Be the blessing of Morrighan to shield us roundward,
Accepting our Beltane blessing from us,
   Accepting our Beltane blessing from us.

***

Blessing the Seed

Blessing the seed before sowing was an important aspect of farming. To quote the Carmina Gadelica page 243 *"Three days before being sown the seed is sprinkled with clear cold water, in the name of Father, and of Son, and of Spirit, the person sprinkling the seed walking sunwise the while. The ritual is picturesque, and is performed with great care and solemnity and, like many of these ceremonies, is a combination of Paganism and Christianity. The moistening of the seed has the effect of hastening its growth when committed to the ground, which is generally begun on a Friday, that day being auspicious for all operations not necessitating the use of iron."*

***

Consecration of the Seed 88

I will go out to sow the seed,

In name of They who gave it growth;

I will place my front in the wind,

And throw a gracious handful on high.

Should a grain fall on a bare rock,

It shall have no soil in which to grow;

As much as falls into the earth,

The dew will make it to be full.

Friday, day auspicious,

The dew will come down to welcome

Every seed that lay in sleep

Since the coming of cold without mercy;

Every seed will take root in the earth,

As the Gods of the elements desired,

The seedling will come forth with the dew,

It will inhale life from the soft wind.

I will come round with my step,

I will go rightways with the sun,

In name of land, of sea, and of sky,

In name of all the gods of Life.

Gracious gods and powers,

Give growth and kindly substance

To every thing that is in my ground,

Till the day of harvest shall come.

The Autumn equinox, day beneficent,

I will put my sickle round about

The root of my corn as was wont;

I will lift the first cut quickly;

I will put it three turns round

My head, saying my rune the while,

My back to the airt of the north;

My face to the fair sun of power.

I shall throw the handful far from me,

I shall close my two eyes twice,

Should it fall in one bunch

My stacks will be productive and lasting;

No girl will come with bad times

To ask a palm bannock from us,

What time rough storms come with frowns

Nor stint nor hardship shall be on us.

***

Maunday Thursday

      Maunday Thursday was a day when those who lived near the ocean made offerings to the God of the sea for a good harvest of both fish and seaweed. Late on Wednesday night the people would gather on the shore and at midnight one man would wade waist deep into the water and offer mead, ale or sometimes porridge into the waves while chanting (Carmichael, 1900). This is an interesting ritual on many levels including the blatantly pagan offering of food or mead to the waves and the timing of the ritual for the liminal moment of midnight. This prayer could still be useful today not only for those who fish or earn their living by the sea, but for anyone who wants to draw abundance to themselves.

Prayer to the Sea *(page 163)*
O Gods of the sea,
Put weed in the drawing wave
To enrich the ground,
To shower on us food.

***

Prayer # 69 would lend itself for use at the summer solstice for those who celebrate it. If that day isn't a Thursday simply substitute the appropriate date and day of the week, for example "the 22nd of June and a Tuesday".

June 9th Prayer 69
The ninth day of June and a Thursday,
Day to send sheep on prosperity,
Day to send cow on calf,
Day to put the web in the warp.

Day to put coracle on the brine,
Day to place the staff to the flag,
Day to bear, day to die,
Day to hunt the heights.

Day to put horses in harness,

Day to send herds to pasture,

Day to make most effective prayer,

Day of my beloved, the Thursday,

    Day of my beloved, the Thursday.

***

Reaping Blessings

    Reaping was a community event that was marked by many different rituals, celebrations, and acts of divination. Carmichael reports that on the first day of the harvest the entire family would dress in their best and process out to the field, where the father of the household would ritually remove his hat, cut some of the corn, and then swing it three times sunwise around his head while chanting a reaping prayer. This prayer would be taken up by the entire family in turn, in thanks to the Power which gave them food, shelter, and blessing in their lives (Carmichael, 1900).

    In the same way as the harvest was begun, it ended with equal ceremony. There are many rituals associated with the end of the harvest, but one method of divination that is mentioned in the Carmina Gadelica is done by the harvesters. After cutting the last sheaf all the sickles and blades would be cast into the air and then the future of the individual reaper would be divined based on how the blade landed (Carmichael, 1900).

These two harvest prayers would work well at Lughnasadh. I can envision either of them as the centerpiece for a Lughnasadh ritual or for use in private devotions on that day. People who choose to celebrate Lughnasadh and the Autumn equinox might like to use one prayer for each holiday. For those who farm they could be said at any point harvesting was being done.

Reaping Blessing 89

Gods may you bless my reaping,
Each ridge, and plain, and field,
Each sickle curved, shapely, hard,

Each ear and handful in the sheaf,
    Each ear and handful in the sheaf.

Bless each maiden and youth,
Each woman and tender child,
Safeguard them beneath Your shield of strength,
And guard them beneath the shadow of Your power,
    Guard them beneath the shadow of Your power.

Encompass each goat, sheep and lamb,
Each cow and horse, and store,
Surround the rocks and herds,
And tend them in a kindly fold,
    Tend them in a kindly fold.

May Lugh, the many skilled, bless us,
May Danu's blessing flow to us,

May Brighid of curling locks bless us,

And our ancestors of the graves and tombs,

    and our ancestors of the graves and tombs.

Reaping Blessing 90

On Tuesday at the rise of the sun,

With the back of the ear of corn to the east,

I will go forth with my sickle under my arm,

And I will reap the harvest of my land.

I will let my sickle down

While the fruitful ear is in my grasp,

I will raise my eye upwards,

I will turn on my heel quickly,

Rightway as travels the sun

From the airt of the east to the west,

From the airt of the north with motion calm

To the very core of the airt of the south.

I will give thanks to the Gods who bless me

For the growing crops of the ground,

Who give food to us and to the flocks

And I will offer the first of my harvest to them.

***

Part Two: Magic

Chapter 14: Success Charms

A river surrounded by trees at Devil's Hopyard in Connecticut

Justice Charms

The person wishing to perform these charms should go before dawn to a place where three streams meet. Just as the sun is rising the person should make a cup of his hands and dip them into the water where the stream meet then wash his face with it, saying the prayer below. Afterwards he should proceed to court and when entering the building should look all around the room then say silently or quietly "Gods bless this place, from floor to roof, my word above every other and the words of all others beneath my feet." (Carmichael, 1900).

Invocation for Justice 20

I will wash my face
In the nine rays of the sun,
As a Goddess washes her Son
    In the rich fermented milk.

Love be in my countenance,
Benevolence in my mind,
Dew of honey in my tongue,
    My breath as the incense.

Black is yonder town,
Black are those therein,
I am the white swan,
    Queen above them.

I will travel in the name of my Gods,

In the likeness of a deer, in the likeness of a horse,

In the likeness of a serpent, in the likeness of a king:

    Stronger will it be with me than with all others.

                            ***

Invocation for Justice 21

Gods, I am bathing my face

In the nine rays of the sun,

As a goddess might bathe her Son

    In generous milk fermented.

Sweetness be in my face,

Riches be in my countenance,

Comb-honey be in my tongue,

    My breath as the incense.

Black is yonder house,

Blacker men therein;

I am the white swan,

    Queen over them.

I will go in the name of my Gods,

In the likeness of a deer, in the likeness of a horse,

In the likeness of a serpent, in the likeness of a king,

    I am more victorious than all others.

                            ***

Victory Charms

The following charms are designed to increase a person's appeal and ensure success at anything that requires speech or persuasion. They could be used well for public speakers, for example. The person using them would go to a place where three streams meet, or otherwise wash with blessed water while reciting the charm.

Prayer for Victory 22

I wash my face
In the nine rays of the sun,
As a goddess might bathe her child
    In the rich fermented milk.

Honey be in my mouth,
Affection be in my face;
The love that Danu gave her children
    Be in the heart of all flesh for me.

All-seeing, all-hearing, all-inspiring may the Gods be,
To satisfy and to strengthen me;
Blind, deaf, and dumb, ever, ever be
    My condemners and my mockers,

The tongue of Ogma in my head,
The eloquence of Ogma in my speech;
The composure of the Sun-faced Lord
    Be mine in presence of the multitude.

Lustration 23

I am washing my face
In the mild rays of the sun,
As a goddess bathes her child
In the rich milk of the cows.

Sweetness be in my mouth,
Wisdom be in my speech,
The love the fair Danu gave Her children
Be in the heart of all flesh for me.

The love of the gods in my heart,
The shield of the gods protecting me,
There is not in sea nor on land
That can overcome the might of my gods.

The hand of Brighid about my neck,
The hand of Danu about my breast,
The hand of Dagda washing me,
The hand of Lugh guarding me.

***

Lustration – variant 23

I am washing my face
In the mild rays of the sun,
As a goddess bathes her child
In the rich milk of the cows.

Force in my mouth,
  Sense in my speech,

The taste of nectar on my lips,
Till I return here again.

The love of the gods in my heart,
The shield of the gods protecting me,
There is not in sea nor on land
That can overcome the might of my gods.

The hand of Brighid about my neck,
The hand of Danu about my breast,
The hand of Dagda washing me,
The hand of Lugh guarding me.

***

Chapter 15: Healing Charms

Amara at Devil's Hopyard in Connecticut 2006

Charms for Mastitis

When performing these charms a sharp object such as a knife or pin should be held towards the body part, you should spit on your fingers and trace a triskele on the area while invoking land, sea, and sky. This follows a common method of folk healing where the illness or injury is threatened as if it were a sentient thing, and ordered to leave the person it is tormenting. All healing charms would be recommended in addition to traditional and alternative medical treatments for the conditions.

Charm 122

See, Blessed Brighid
The breast of this mother is swollen:
May you give peace to this breast
May you subdue the swelling;

May you give peace to this breast
May you subdue the swelling.
I see it myself, Brighid,
The suffering of this mother
May you appease this breast,
May you subdue the swelling;

May you appease this breast,
May you subdue the swelling.
See, Healing Goddess

Midwife of all mothers,

May you appease this breast,
May you subdue the swelling;

May you appease this breast,
May you subdue the swelling
Brighid sees the suffering
And she does what is needed
She gives ease to the breast
And rest to the swelling;
She gives ease to the breast
And rest to the swelling

Charm 123   *(use for humans or livestock)*

You red swelling, tight and deadly,
Leave that part and spot
There is the udder in the ground,
And leave the breast
See, Dian Cecht, the woman
And her breast so swollen,
See her as well Airmed, Daughter of gentle healing
You red swelling, deadly and growing
Leave the breast and the spot,
remove yourself, go away,
Healed is the breast,
relieved is the swelling

Flee thieving redness,
Flee quickly milk thief
Swelling that was in the breast
Leave the udder and the breast
And flee quickly.

***

Charm for Dental Issues

This is a modified charm for a toothache. Originally the Carmina Gadelica version involves using water from a specific holy well with specific actions. I would bless some water, then chant this over the water, hold up a cup of the water, repeat the chant, take a mouthful of water, swish and spit, then repeat the chant a third time.

***

Charm for a Toothache 126

The incantation put by Brighid
Before the Mother of the Gods,
On sea, on ocean, on coast.
For painful aching teeth.

The pain that tortured me,
In these teeth in my head,
Agony hard with my teeth,
This agony distressing me.

I put this pain far from me;
As long as I myself shall last
May my teeth last in my head.

***

Charms for Sprains and Broken Bones

These could be used for sprains, broken bones, or lacerations. In addition to any necessary medical care, hold your hands over the afflicted area and chant the healing charm. For slow healing injuries I would recommend repeating the charm on a daily basis until the injury is totally healed.

Charm of the Sprain 130

Brighid went out
Early in the morning,
With a pair of horses;
One sprained his leg,
With much suffering
And separation,
She put bone to bone,
She put flesh to flesh,
She put sinew to sinew,
She put vein to vein;
As she healed that
May I heal this.

Charm for a Sprain 131

High King Nuada lost an arm,
Sprained is this limb before me;
Nuada became whole once more,
May this limb also be whole.

As that was made whole
May this become whole,
As I will it to be so now,
Through the sovereignty of Nuada,
And three healing gods of the Aos Sidhe.
By High King Nuada,
Dian Cecht, Airmed and Miach

***

Charm for a Broken Bone 132

Dian Cecht went out
Early in the morning,
He found the legs of the horses
In broken fragments;
He put marrow to marrow,
He put pith to pith,
He put bone to bone,
He put membrane to membrane,
He put tendon to tendon,
He put blood to blood,

He put tallow to tallow,

He put flesh to flesh,

He put fat to fat,

He put skin to skin,

He put hair to hair,

He put warm to warm,

He put cool to cool,

As the God of Healing healed that

It is in His nature to heal this,

If it be His own will to do it.

    Through the powers of life,

    And of the Three Gods of healing.

***

Charms for Urinary Issues

These deal with blood in urine and other kidney issues, originally with animals so I have rewritten two of them slightly for use with people. They could be used for any medical issue affecting the kidneys. There are two options that I would suggest for use of these charms in people; either hold your hands over the person's mid-back and chant the charm or else chant the charm over a drink of water or perhaps cranberry juice and then have the afflicted person drink the charged liquid.

To Remove Blood from Urine 180

By the tides of the eternal sea,

by the bedrock of the firm earth,

by the ceaseless winds of sky,

So shall this be.

Great wave, red wave,

strength of sea, strength of ocean

the nine wells of Mac Lyr

to pour help on you

Put a stop to the blood,

Put a flood to the urine

A Red Water Charm, for Blood in Urine of Animals 181

I am now on the plain,

Reducing wrath and fury,

Making the charm of the red water,

    To the beauteous black cow.

For milk, for milk substance, for milk produce,

For whisked whey, for milk riches,

For curdled milk, for milk plenty,

    For butter, for cheese, for curds.

For progeny and prosperity,

For rutting time and rutting,

For desire and cattle,

    For passion and prosperity.

The nine wells of Mac Lyr,

May relief be poured on you,

blood be stopped,

Urine be freed,

    You cow of cows, black cow.

Great sea,

Red cascade,

Stop blood,

Flow urine.

***

To Remove Kidney Infection with Bleeding 182

I have a charm for kidney infection,

for the disease that is invasive

I have a charm for blood in urine,

for the disease which is painful.

As a river runs cold

as a mill grinds quickly,

Brighid, blessed goddess of healing,

cease the blood and heal the kidneys.

By the power of land, sea, and sky,

so shall it be

***

Charm for Tumors

    This is the only charm which does not come from the Gadelica. I've used it before for cancer patients with success, and so have chosen to include it here. It is a heavily rewritten version of a Pow-wow chant; I would recommend the book <u>Pow-wows, or Long Lost Friend</u> for more on this school of folk magic.

The charm should be chanted while holding your hands over the afflicted area, or a picture of the person. I highly recommend doing this charm on a set regular basis, for example three times a day for a series of nine or 27 days. In order for the charm to be effective it must be done often and consistently.

A Charm to Reduce and Heal Tumors

Nine waves upon the ocean
The nine become eight,
The eight become seven,
The seven become six,
The six become five,
The five become four,
The four become three,
The three become two,
The two become one,
One becomes none;
Out from the marrow into the blood,
Out from the blood into the flesh,
Out from the flesh into the skin,
Out from the skin into the hair,
Out from the hair to the healing earth.

***

This is a livestock specific charm, for a horse suffering from strangles, it could also work for a horse in colic. I would suggest chanting it while standing next to the animal, but if necessary over a picture or while visualizing the animal should also work.

<u>The Strangles Charm 183</u>

'Here is a horse in strangles,'
Said Airmid.

'I will turn it,'
Said Dian Cecht.

'This very morning? '
Said Airmid.

' Before the sun rises again,'
Said Dian Cecht.

'Three pillars are in the well,'
Said Airmid.

'I will lift them,'
Said Dian Cecht.

'Will that heal him?'
asked Miach.

'Assuredly,'
Said Dian Cecht.

***

This next charm is also designed for animals with digestive issues, although this one is not horse specific.

Indigestion Charm 189 *(for animals)*

The spell made by Airmed,
To the one cow of the woman,
For the sore mouth, for the gum disease,
For the bag, for the swelling,
For the indigestion;

For the flux disease,
For the cud disease,
For the stomach disease,
For the digestion disease,
For the surfeit;

For the painful disease,
For the cramping disease,
For the water disease,
For the red disease,
For the madness;

I will cleave the sore mouth,
I will cleave the gum disease,
I will cleave the bag,
I will cleave the swelling,
And I will kill the indigestion;

I will cleave the flux,
I will cleave the cud,

I will cleave the stomach,

I will cleave the digestion,

And drive away the surfeit;

I will cleave the pain,

I will cleave the cramping,

I will cleave the water,

I will cleave the red,

And the madness will wither.

***

Much of the Gadelica deals with charms for animals. This particular charm is intended for livestock that chew cud; however I can see an easy application here for people with stomach issues and so am taking the liberty to re-write a second version for human use. This version will be modified quite a bit, but I believe it will be useful and maintain the spirit of the original

Indigestion Charm 189   *(for people)*

The spell made by Airmed,

To the person suffering,

For the flu, for the sore throat,

For the ache, for the swelling,

For the indigestion;

For the flux disease,

For the vomiting disease,

For the stomach disease,

For the digestion disease,

For the over-indulgence;

For the painful disease,

For the cramping disease,

For the water disease,

For the feverish disease,

For the suffering;

I will cleave the flu,

I will cleave the sore throat,

I will cleave the ache,

I will cleave the swelling,

And I will kill the indigestion;

I will cleave the flux,

I will cleave the vomiting,

I will cleave the stomach,

I will cleave the digestion,

And drive away the over-indulgence;

I will cleave the pain,

I will cleave the cramping,

I will cleave the water,

I will cleave the feverishness,

And the suffering will wither.

***

Swan Lullaby

Swans are birds of especially good omen. To hear one is good luck, more so if it is on a Tuesday morning before eating breakfast, or when seeing seven or multiples of seven. Often swans are believed to be maidens transformed into the shape of swans and so killing one is a grave offense to the community. The following charm is a healing one, written in the form of a lullaby which would be sung to an ailing child. It is said to be based on a tale where a woman nursed an ailing swan back to health and found her sick child's health restored as well (Carmichael, 1900).

In modern use this healing charm would be especially good for use on children. I would recommend singing or chanting it over the ill child; however as always if this is not feasible than doing so over a picture or while visualizing the child should also work. I think this charm may also be useful as a chant to create a talisman for an ill child, by chanting the charm over a stuffed swan toy then giving the toy to the sick child to aid in healing. In this way the toy swan would act as a symbolic representation of the swan in the story is being petitioned to heal the child.

Lullaby 211

Oh, white swan,
    Hu hi! ho ho!

Sad your condition,
    Hu hi! ho ho!

Pitiful your state,

    Hu hi! ho ho!

Your blood is flowing,

    Hu hi! ho ho!

    Hu hi! ho ho!

Oh white swan,

    Hu hi! ho ho!

Far from your friends,

    Hu hi! ho ho!

Lady of your converse,

    Hu hi! ho ho!

Remain near me,

    Hi hi! ho ho!

    Hu hi! ho ho!

You healer of gladness,

    Hu hi! ho ho!

Bless my little child,

    Hu hi! ho ho!

Shield him from death,

    Hu hi! ho ho!

Hasten him to health,

    Hu hi! ho ho!

As you desire,
> Hu hi! ho ho!
> Hu hi! hi ho!

Pain and sorrow
> Hu hi! ho ho!

To your injurer,
> Hu hi! ho ho!
> Hu hi! hi ho!

A thousand welcomes to you,
> Hu hi! ho ho!

Life and health be yours,
> Hu hi! ho ho!

The age of joy be yours,
> Hu hi! ho ho!

In every place,
> Hu hi! ho ho!
> Hu hi! hi ho!

Peace and growth to him,
> Hu hi! ho ho!

Strength and worth to him,
> Hu hi! ho ho!

Victory of place,
> Hu hi! ho ho!

Everywhere to him,
> Hu hi! ho ho!
> Hu hi! hi ho!

Blessed Danu,
> Hu hi! ho ho!

Fair white lovely,
> Hu hi! ho ho!

Cuddling you,
> Hu hi! ho ho!

Hugging you,
> Hu hi! ho ho!

Bathing you,
> Hu hi! ho ho!

Be with you,
> Hu hi! ho ho!

Shielding you
> Hu hi! ho ho!

From the net of your enemy;
> Hu hi! ho ho!
> Hu hi! ho ho!

Caressing you,
> Hu hi! ho ho!

Guarding you,
> Hu hi! ho ho!

Fulfilling you
>   Hu hi! ho ho!

The love of your mother,
>   Hu hi! ho ho!

The love of her love,
>   Hu hi! ho ho!

The love of the spirits,
>   Hu hi! ho ho!

And the gods of life!
>   Hu hi! ho ho!
>   Hu hi! hi ho!

***

Chapter 16: Protection Charms

A frog – by nature a liminal creature

This first charm is a protection charm to be said while weaving cloth, which may also be used for any type of sewing, to pray for protection on the person who will wear the item. The intent is that the item woven or sown would then act as a protective talisman for the wearer. To make the charm, repeatedly say either aloud or silently the prayer while working on the cloth Normally I would suggest repeating it three or nine times each time the material was worked, however given the rune's emphasis on the number seven I think repeating it seven times would have the greatest effect.

Consecration of the Cloth 113

Well can I say my rune,
Descending with the glen;
    One rune,
    Two runes,
    Three runes,
    Four runes,
    Five runes,
    Six runes.
    Seven runes,
    Seven and a half runes,
    Seven and a half runes.

May the person of this clothing never be wounded,
May he never be torn;
What time he goes into battle or combat,

May the sanctuary shield of the Gods be his.
What time he goes into battle or combat,
May the sanctuary shield of the Gods be his.

This is not second clothing and it is not worn-out,
Nor is it the rightful property of another.

Cresses green culled beneath a stone,
And given to a woman in secret.
The shank of the deer in the head of the herring,
And in the slender tail of the speckled salmon.

***

The following is one of the Fath-Fith charms; below is my version which required very little reworking. I substituted what I feel are appropriate goddess names for the Christian Mary and St. Bride, others might adapt this with different names or by removing the names entirely. This charm should be chanted or repeated silently in order to make something unnoticed, or apparently invisible, to others. If using on one's self simply change the pronouns.

From the Carmina Gadelica, Volume 2, page 22:

"'FĀTH-FĪTH' and 'fīth-fāth' are interchangeable terms and indiscriminately used. They are applied to the occult power which rendered a person invisible to mortal eyes and which transformed one object into another. Men and women were made invisible, or men were transformed into horses, bulls, or stags, *while women were transformed into cats, hares, or hinds. These transmutations were sometimes voluntary, sometimes involuntary. The 'fīth-fāth' was especially serviceable to hunters, warriors, and travelers, rendering them invisible or unrecognizable to enemies and to animals."*

Fath Fith 133

"Fath fith

I will make on you,

By Mórríghan of the augury,

By Brighid of the corslet,

From sheep, from ram,

From goat, from buck,

From fox, from wolf,

From sow, from boar,

From dog, from cat,

From hipped-bear,

From wilderness-dog,

From watchful 'scan,'

From cow, from horse,

From bull, from heifer,

From daughter, from son,

From the birds of the air,

From the creeping things of the earth,

From the fish of the sea,

From the spirits of the storm."

Charms for Lasting Life

This is a type of protective charm from the Carmina Gadelica used to keep the person or animal it is set on from physical harm. The first charm needed serious re-writing to re-paganize it so I am offering two versions, one with the Christian references removed, and the other with them replaced so that people will be able to choose the one they are most comfortable using. The second version is open to substitution of different God or Goddess names, based on individual circumstances.

From the Carmina Gadelica, Volume 2, page 26,

"'SIAN' or 'seun' is occult agency, supernatural power used to ward away injury, and to protect invisibly. Belief in the charm was common, and examples of its efficacy are frequently told."

Sian a Bheatha Bhuan - A Charm of Lasting Life 134 *Version 1*

I place the charm on your body,

And on your prosperity,

For your protection.

Between sole and throat,

Between breast-bone and knee,

Between back and front,

Between chest and sole,

Between eye and hair.

No blade shall cut you,
No sea shall drown you,
No woman shall wile you,
No man shall wound you.

From the crown of your head
To the soles of your feet.

The charm of lasting life is on you now,
You shall never know disgrace.

You shall go forth in safety.

You shall come back in safety.

To the Powers of life you now belong wholly,

I place this charm early on Monday,
In passage hard, brambly, thorny,
Go out with the charm about your body,
And have no fear.

You will ascend the crest of the hill,
Protected you will be behind,
You are the calm swan in battle,
Preserved you will be amidst the slaughter,
You can stand against five hundred,
And your oppressors shall be seized.

***

Version 2

I place the charm on your body,

And on your prosperity,

The charm of the Gods of life

For your protection.

The charm that Brighid of the cattle

Put round the fair neck of Dornghil,

Between sole and throat,

Between breast-bone and knee,

Between back and front,

Between chest and sole,

Between eye and hair.

The sword of Lugh on your side,

The shield of Lugh on your shoulder,

There is nothing between sky and earth,

nor earth and sea that can overcome you.

No blade shall cut you,

No sea shall drown you,

No woman shall wile you,

No man shall wound you.

The mantle of Brighid about you,

The shadow of the Mórríghan above you,

Protected from the crown of your head

To the soles of your feet.

The charm of lasting life is on you now,
You will never know disgrace.

You shall go forth in safety,
You shall come back in safety,
To the Gods of life you now belong wholly,
And to all the Powers together.

I place this charm early on Monday,
In passage hard, brambly, thorny,
Go out with the charm about your body,
And have no fear.

You shall ascend the crest of the hill,
Protected you will be behind,
You are the calm swan in battle,
Preserved you will be amidst the slaughter,
You can stand against five hundred,
And your oppressors shall be seized.

>   The charm of lasting life is on you!
>   The arms of the Gods are around you!

***

This second charm is aimed at preventing harm to livestock and did not require much alteration. It could easily be adapted further for use on any animal, including small house pets by simply changing the second line slightly.

A Charm Of Lasting Life 135

I will place the charm of the lasting life,

Upon your cattle active, broad, and full,

The knoll upon which the herds shall lie down,

    That they may rise from it whole and well.

That they lay down with success, and with blessing,

That they get up with activity and following,

And without envy, without malice, without ill-will,

Without small eye, without large eye,

    Without the five eyes of neglect.

I will pull this away, the envious vein

On the head of the house, and the family,

That every evil trait, and every evil tendency

    shall be cast out and returned to those who sent it.

    If tongue cursed you,

    A heart blessed you;

    If eye blighted you,

    A wish prospered you.

A hurly-burlying, a topsy-turvying,

A hard hollying and a wan withering

To their female sheep and to their male calves,

    For the nine and the nine score years.

                  ***

This charm is intended as a magical fox-repellant, to protect sheep, but it would work equally well for protection of any animal foxes like to target.

The Spell of the Fox 184

I cast the spell of the wood dog,
On the feet of the fox,
On his heart, on his liver,
On his gullet of greediness,
On his surpassing pointed teeth,
On the bend of his stomach.

Be this charm upon the sheep-kind,
The charm of Brighid kindly-white, mild-white,
The charm of Brighid lovely-fair, tender-fair,
Against dogs, against birds, against man-kind,
Against fairy dogs, against world dogs,
From here and from there.

***

A good basic cattle protection charm:

The Charm of the Cattlefold 185

I drive the cattle within
The gateway of the herds,
On voice of the dead,
On voice of the bull,
On voice of the pairing,
On voice of the grayling cow

White-headed, strong-headed, abundant of udder.

Without ceasing, without decreasing,

Be the big stone of the base of the couple

As a full-weighted tether

Trailing from the hunch of your rump,

Till bright daylight comes in to-morrow.

The gods of life watch over you,

Save you, and shield you, and tend you,

Until I or mine shall meet you again.

***

Chapter 17: Love Charms

Wild fern and mint

These two charms use a series of herbal ingredients along with a specific set of preparations instead of a spoken chant. This charm also included ingredients that require substitution; the charm calls for three bones from the body of an old man. As explained in a note from the Gadelica, *"The lucky bones are the joint of the big toe of the right foot and the nail-joints of the left foot of an old man."* (Carmichael, 1900).

Since I don't advocate disturbing graves or abusing corpses, I recommend substituting three apple twigs for the mentioned bones and have changed the lines of the charm accordingly. Apple is a tree with a long history relating to love magic and charms.

Love Charm 138

It is not love knowledge to you
To draw water through a reed,
But the love of him [her] you have chosen,
With his [her] warmth to draw to you.

Get up early on Sunday,
To the broad flat flag
Take with you Foxglove
And the Butterbur

Lift them on your shoulder
In a wooden shovel,
Get nine stems of ferns
Cut with an axe,

And three twigs of apple,

That have been found on the ground,

Burn them together on a fire,

And make them all into ashes.

Shake it over the heart of your lover,

Against the sting of the north wind,

And I will pledge, and warrant you,

That man [woman] will never leave you.

Love Charm 139

A love charm for you,

Water drawn through a straw,

The warmth of him [her] that you love,

    With love to draw to you.

Arise early on Sunday,

To the flat rock of the shore

Take with you Butterbur

    And the cap of a Foxglove

A small quantity of embers

carried securely,

A special handful of sea-weed

    In a wooden shovel.

Three twigs of apple wood,

Newly found on the earth,

Nine stalks of fern,

    Newly trimmed with an axe.

Burn them on a fire of sticks

And make them all into ashes;

Sprinkle over the heart of your lover,

    Against the venom of the north wind.

Go round the fort of procreation,

The circuit of the five turns,

And I will vow and warrant to you

    That man [woman] will never leave you.

***

Chapter 18: For the Evil Eye

This series of charms from the Carmina Gadelica all deal with the evil eye, that is the curse laid upon a person by another who wishes them ill or looks upon them with envy. This first one is my personal favorite; I love the imagery it presents and find it reminiscent of the Song of Amergin. Anyone who has read the works of the witch Sibyl Leek may recognize the middle portion of the charm, the "power over" section, as she made use of this portion in an unhexing spell in one of her books, clearly drawing on the Gadelica as a source. That same section has also appeared in a young adult novel by L. J. Smith called <u>The Power</u>; all of which could be seen as a testament to the power and flexibility of the Carmina Gadelica charms, as well as their intrinsic value.

<u>Exorcism of the Evil Eye 141</u>

I trample upon the evil eye,
As the duck tramples upon the lake,
As the swan tramples upon the water,
As the horse tramples upon the plain,
As the cow tramples upon the grass,
As the host tramples the sky,
   As the host tramples the air.

Power of wind I have over it,
Power of wrath I have over it,
Power of fire I have over it,
Power of thunder I have over it,
Power of lightning I have over it,

Power of storms I have over it,

Power of moon I have over it,

Power of sun I have over it,

Power of stars I have over it,

Power of earth I have over it,

Power of sky and of the worlds I have over it,

Power of the sky and of the worlds I have over it.

A portion of it upon the grey stones,

A portion of it upon the steep hills,

A portion of it upon the fast falls,

A portion of it upon the fair meadows,

And a portion upon the great salt sea,

She herself is the best instrument to carry it,

    The great salt sea,

    is the best instrument to carry it.

In the names of the Three of Life,

In the names of the Gods of Skill,

In the names of all the Ancient Ones,

And of the Powers together.

***

    This second charm had to be reworked the most; I have altered a section to call on some of the Irish gods in place of Christian saints but others may choose to simply eliminate this section instead or use an alternate charm. This charm may be particularly useful in dealing with gossip and malicious rumors as well as unwanted romantic attentions. The charm references a thread "*going round you*" so I would suggest using an actual physical thread or cord to wrap yourself or the person the charm is being said for. After saying the charm keep the thread somewhere safe. As always alter any nouns or pronouns as needed if saying the charm for yourself.

Counteracting the Evil Eye 142

An evil eye covered you,
A mouth spoke of you,
A heart envied you,
A mind desired you.

Four have done you harm
Man and wife,
Youth and maiden;
Three will I send to thwart them,

I appeal to Danu,
Mother of the aos sidhe,
I appeal to Brighid,
Healer, Poet and Smith,
I appeal to Manannán,

God of wave and sea,
And I appeal to the Otherworld,
To all helpfully inclined spirits.

If it be a man that has done you harm,
With evil eye,
With evil wish,
With evil passion,

May you cast off each ill,
Every malignity,
Every malice,
Every harassment,
And may you be well for ever,
While this thread
Goes round you,
In honor of the Powers of Life,
And of the Gods above.

***

    This charm has two purposes, to bless the person who has been afflicted with the evil eye and to send the eye back on whoever sent it to you. I advise caution when using any charm or spell that aims to return a curse or negative energy to the source unless you are very sure there is a definite human source to return it to. Otherwise it may be possible to magnify what is a naturally occurring situation by feeding energy into it. It is also important not to direct the energy at anyone specifically, even if you think you know who is causing you grief, but rather simply direct the energy to return to its source. If you are wrong about who is sending this on you it is possible to make the situation far more complicated by sending the energy on to an innocent third party whom you blame while leaving the actual source free to continue sending the evil eye on you. This is why it is better with spells such as #143 to let the energy find its own way home and not allow yourself to direct it.

Spell for the Evil Eye 143

The fair spell that was sent,
Over stream, over sea, over land,
Against incantations, against withering glance,
Against inimical power,
Against the teeth of wolf,
Against the testicles of wolf,
Against the three crooked cranes,
And against the three crooked bones,
Whoever made the eye against you,
May it lie upon him,
May it lie upon his house,
May it lie upon his flocks,
May it lie upon his substance,
May it lie upon his fatness,
May it lie upon his means,
May it lie upon his children,
May it lie upon his wife,
May it lie upon his descendants.

I will subdue the eye,
I will suppress the eye,
And I will banish the eye,

The three evils inviting,

And the tongue of death completely.

Three lovely spirits,

Born with the world,

If they remain, then life will stay with you.

***

Much like the previous charm this one aims to send energy back on the one who has sent the evil eye to you. Use with similar caution.

<u>Charm for the Evil Eye 145</u>

Whoever laid the eye on you,

May it lie upon him,

May it lie upon his house,

May it lie upon his flocks,

On the shuffling old woman,

On the sour-faced old woman,

On the bounding old woman,

On the sharp-shinned old woman,

Who arose in the morning,

With her eye on her flocks,

With her flocks in her field,

May she never own a fold,

May she never have half her desires,

The part of her which the ravens do not eat,

May the birds devour.

Four made the eye at you,

Man and woman, youth and maiden;

Three who will cast the envy off you,

Three Gods of great power.

As the fruit is lifted

From the branches of the bushes,

Lifted from you shall be

Every ailment, every envy, every jealousy,

From this day until the last day of your life.

***

Charm #146 is a cure for the evil eye. It is used to remove the negative energy that has been sent from a person. This is probably one of the best general charms to remove the evil eye.

<u>A Charm 146</u>

I arise to make the charm,

    Against the keen-eyed men,

    Against the peering-eyed women,

    Against the slim, slender, fairy-darts,

    Against the swift arrows of fury.

Two made on you the withered eye,

Man and woman with venom and envy,

Three whom I will set against them,

    three gods of great power.

Four and twenty diseases in the constitution of man and beast,

Powers scrape them, Powers search them, Powers cleanse them,

From your blood, from your flesh, from your gentle bones,

From this day until your days on earth are done.

***

Spell Of the Eye 150

I place this spell to my eye,

As the Powers of life ordained,

Spell of Lugh, many skilled god,

Spell of Brighid, tranquil of the cattle,

Spell of Danu, mother of many,

Spell of cows, spell of herds,

Spell of sheep, spell of flocks,

Spell of greatness, spell of means,

Spell of joy, spell of peace,

Spell of war, spell of the brave,

The third best spell under the sun,

The powerful spell of the Three Powers.

***

This is a spell to remove the evil eye, but it could also be used as a general blessing or to call in positive energy.

Spell of the Eye 151

The spell fair-white I send,

Here to the mainland,

Here to the coastland,

Here on the lake,

Here on the ocean,

To thwart eye,

To thwart net,

To thwart envy,

To thwart hate.

To repel illness,

To repel sickness,

To repel swelling,

To repel infection.

***

This spell for the evil eye is another one that aims to send the energy back to whoever placed it on the person originally and so, as always, should be used with care.

Spell for the Eye 152

I send to you the spell the was sent

To Brighid the lovely and fair,

For sea, for land, for water, and for withering glance,

For teeth of wolf, for aggression of wolf.

Whoever laid the eye on you,

May it oppress him,

May it oppress his house,

May it oppress his flocks.

Let me subdue the eye,

Let me avert the eye,

The three complete tongues of fullness,

In the arteries of the heart,

   In the vitals of the navel.

***

     Charm # 193 was collected by Carmichael from a woman he called a Scottish gypsy. It is by far the strongest and harshest charm in this book and should be used with extreme caution. Its purpose is nothing less than to kill, after much suffering, those who have harmed the person. The way it is written it could be used for those who have been physically attacked: assaulted, raped, or otherwise seriously injured, and have no legal recourse.

A Charm for Those Who Would Harm Me 193

The wicked who would do me harm

May he take the throat disease,

Around and around, spirally, circularly,

Fluxy, pellety, horny-grim.

May it be harder than the stone,

May it be blacker than the coal,

May it be swifter than the duck,

May it be heavier than the lead.

May it be fiercer, sharper, harsher, more malignant,

Than the hard, wound-quivering holly,

May it be more sour than the blessed, lustrous, bitter, salt,

seven times seven times.

Oscillating there,

Undulating here,

Staggering downwards,

Floundering upwards.

Drivelling outwards,

Snivelling inwards,

Oft hurrying out,

Seldom coming in.

A wisp the portion of each hand,

A foot in the base of each pillar,

A leg the prop of each jamb,

A flux driving and dragging him.

A dysentery of blood from heart, from form, from bones,

From the liver, from the lobe, from the lungs,

And a searching of veins, of throat, and of kidneys,

To my attackers and traducers.

In name of the Gods of might,

Who warded from me every evil,

And who shielded me in strength,

From the net of my breakers

    And destroyers.

Chapter 19: Herbal and Blessing Charms

White clover

Chapter 19 deals with charms aimed at blessing and increasing luck in a person's life. Many of these charms are based on finding, collecting, and preserving specific herbs.

In spell # 153, you would want to find the yarrow and then recite the charm while harvesting a small amount. Be careful while harvesting to do no unnecessary harm to the plant and take only what you need. Also when these charms talk about cattle and milk I tend to see them in a non-pastoral setting as metaphors for abundance and plenty. The lines can stand as they are if you take this approach, or if you prefer you could adjust them

Spell of Counteracting 153

I will pluck the gracious yarrow
That Brighid plucked with her hand.

The gracious Lady of Healing
Came with her lovely face above me.

Bright Brighid came towards me,
With milk, with substance, with produce,
With female calves, with milk product.

In names of the Gods of life
Supply me with your abundance,
The blessings of the Lady of the well
To put milk in udder and gland,
With female calves, with progeny.

May you have the length of seven years
Without loss of calf, without loss of milk,
Without loss of means or of dear friends.

***

There is some debate as to what, exactly the "*Red-stalk*" is but the three leading theories are Aster, Robert Geranium, and Sheep Sorrell. Although it would be best to identify the specific plant with certainty, I believe that any of these possibilities would be successful if picked while chanting the charm.

The Red Stalk 157

I will pluck the little red-stalk of surety,

The lint the lovely Brighid drew through her hands,
For success of health, for success of friendship,
    For success of joyousness,
For overcoming of evil mind, for overcoming of evil eye,
    For overcoming of bewitchment,
For overcoming of evil deed, for overcoming of evil conduct,
    For overcoming of malediction,
For overcoming of evil news, for overcoming of evil words,
    For success of blissfulness--
    For success of blissfulness.

***

A charm to increase prosperity using ivy. This is an interesting one because it specifies a time period "a year and a day" that it seems the charm is meant to stay in effect. With that being the case I would recommend making this a seasonal tradition and refreshing the charm at the same time each year.

The Tree-entwining Ivy 158

I will pluck the tree-entwining ivy,

As Airmed plucked with her gentle hand,

As the Powers of life have ordained,

To put milk in udder and gland,

With speckled fair female calves,

As was spoken in the prophecy,

On this foundation for a year and a day,

Through the hearts of the Gods of life, and of all the powers.

***

The following three charms involve chanting while picking the Figwort. They are designed to ensure blessing and prosperity, as seen in an abundance of milk and calves based on the location and appearance of this plant.

To quote the Carmina Gadelica, Volume 2, page 78 *"'The "torranan" is a blessed plant. It grows in sight of the sea. Its root is a cluster of four bulbs like the four teats of a cow. The stalk of the plant is as long as the arm, and the bloom is as large as the breast of a woman, and as pure white as the driven snow of the hill. It is full of the milk of grace and goodness and of the gift of peace and power, and fills with the filling and ebbs with the ebbing tide. It is therefore meet to cull the plant with the flow and not with the ebb of the restless sea. If I had the "torranan" it would ensure to me abundant milk in my cow all the year."*

The Charm of the Figwort 159

I will pluck the figwort,

With the produce of sea and land,

The plant of joy and gladness,

The plant of rich milk.

As the Powers of life ordained,

To put milk in pap and gland,

As the Gods of life ordained,

To place substance in udder and kidney,

With milk, with milkiness, with butter milk,

With produce, with whisked whey, with milk-product,

With speckled female calves,

And without male calves,

With progeny, with joy, with produce,

With love, with charity, with bounty,

Without man of evil wish,

Without woman of evil eye,

Without malice, without envy, without poverty,

Without wild bear,

Without wilderness dog,

Without aggression of wolf,

Obtaining hold of the rich dainty

    Into which this shall go.

Figwort of bright lights,

Produce to draw here,

With fruit, with grace, with joy.

***

The Figwort 160

I will pluck the figwort,

With the fullness of sea and land,

At the flow, not the ebb of the tide,

By your hand gentle Airmed.

The kindly Miach directing me,

The wise Daghda protecting me,

While Brighid, benefit of women,

Shall put produce in the cattle.

As the Powers of life ordained,

To put milk in breast and gland,

As the Gods of life ordained,

To put flow in udder and teat.

In udder of ewe,

In udder of goat,

In udder of sow,

In udder of mare.

In udder of sow,

In udder of heifer,

In udder of goat, ewe, and sheep,

Of deer, and of cow.

With milk, with cream, with substance,

With rutting, with begetting, with fruitfulness,

With female calves excelling,

With progeny, with joy, with blessing.

Without man of evil wish,

Without woman of evil eye,

Without malice, without envy,

Without one evil.

In name of the Gods of life,

In name of the Mother of the Gods,

In name of Brighid herself.

***

The Charm of the Figwort 161

I will gather the figwort,

Of a thousand blessings, of a thousand virtues,

The calm Brighid endowing it to me,

The fair Airmed enriching it to me,

Came the nine joys,

With the nine waves,

To gather the figwort,

Of a thousand blessings, of a thousand virtues--

Of a thousand blessings, of a thousand virtues.

The arm of Airmed about me,

The face of Airmed before me,

The mantle of Airmed over me,

My noble plant is being gathered--
My noble plant is being gathered.

In name of the Father of Wisdom,
In name of the Red God of Knowledge,
In name of the Good God,
Who in the struggles of my life,
Will not leave me on my own
   Who in the struggles of my life,
   Will not leave me on my own.

***

In this next charm the Fairy Wort is most likely the Cowslip. Finding, collecting and keeping this flower is especially potent against gossip and slander, but also acts as an overall blessing for the possessor.

The Fairy Wort 162

I will pick the fairy wort,

With expectation from the fairy bower,
To overcome every oppression,
As long as it be fairy wort.

Fairy wort, fairy wort,
I envy the one who has you,
There is nothing the sun encircles,
But is to her a sure victory.

Pluck will I the honored plant
Plucked by the great Airmed, who knows all herbal wisdom,
To cast off me every tale of scandal and flippancy,
Ill-life, ill-love, ill-luck,
Hatred, falsity, fraud and vexation,
Till I go in the cold grave beneath the sod.

These next two are more yarrow charms, intended to make a woman more attractive and less susceptible to men's charms.

Interestingly in lines 7 through 10 of the first charm the woman associates herself with sea, land, sky and the tree, before declaring her strength and dominance.

The Yarrow 163

I will pluck the yarrow fair,
That my face shall be more gentle,
That my lips shall be more warm,
That my speech shall be more chaste,
 My speech will be the beams of the sun,
My lips will be the juice of the strawberry.

May I be an isle in the sea,
May I be a hill on the shore,
May I be a star in the waning of the moon,
May I be a staff to the weak,
I can wound every man,
No man can wound me.

The Yarrow 164

I will pluck the yarrow fair,

That more brave shall be my hand,

That more warm shall be my lips,

That more swift shall be my foot;

May I be an island at sea,

May I be a rock on land,

That I can afflict any man,

   Yet no man can afflict me.

***

St. John's Wort, also called St. Columba's Plant, is held in high regard to this day. It is traditionally picked and worn beneath the left arm (Carmichael, 1900).

The Carmina Gadelica, Volume 2 page 96: *"Saint John's Wort is one of the few plants still cherished by the people to ward away second-sight, enchantment, witchcraft, evil eye, and death, and to ensure peace and plenty in the house, increase and prosperity in the fold, and growth and fruition in the field. The plant is secretly secured in the bodices of the women and in the vests of the men, under the left armpit. Saint John's Wort, however, is effective only when the plant is accidentally found."*

The above quote mentions a curious belief – that these charms are only effective when the plant they use is found accidently. It would behoove anyone interested in using these herbal charms to learn to identify any plants of interest in the wild and to keep a sharp eye out for them. When you are fortunate enough to find any given plant growing wild, and choose to collect it, remember to say the charm as you harvest the plant.

Saint John's Wort Charm 165

I will pick my little plant,
As a prayer to my gods,
To quiet the wrath of men of blood,
To check the wiles of wanton women.

I will pick my little plant,
As a prayer to my gods,
That its power will be mine
Over all I see.

I will pick my little plant,
As a prayer to the Three Gods of Skill,
Beneath the blessing of the gods of life,
And of Danu, mother of the ancient people.

***

St. Columba's Plant Charm 166

I will pluck what I have found,
In communion with my gods,
To stop the wiles of wily men,
    And the arts of foolish women.

I will pluck my sacred plant,
As a prayer to my gods,

That mine be the power of this sacred plant,

    Over every one I see.

I will pluck the leaf above,

As ordained of the High King,

In name of the Three,

    And of Danu, Mother of a skilled people.

***

St. Columba's Plant Charm 167

Little plant of blessing,

Without seeking, without searching,

Little plant of blessing,

Under my arm forever!

For luck of men,

For luck of means,

For luck of wishing,

For luck of sheep,

For luck of goats,

For luck of birds,

For luck of fields,

For luck of sea-bounty,

For luck of fish,

For luck of produce and cattle,

For luck of progeny and people,

For luck of battle and victory,

On land, on sea, on ocean,

Through the Three realms,
Through the Three powers,
Through the Three elements,
Little plant of blessing,
I pick you now,
    I pick you now.

***

St. John's Wort Charm 168

Saint John's Wort, Saint John's Wort,
I envy whoever has you,
I will pluck you with my right hand,
I will preserve you with my left hand,
Whoever finds you in the cattle fold,
Shall never be without prosperity.

***

    From page 106 of Volume 2 of the Carmina Gadelica *"some people say that the lucky shamrock has four leaves, other say five, but all agree it must be found by chance not sought out intentionally. Once found it is preserved as a peerless talisman."*

    Charm #170 references seven joys, including health, friends, cattle, sheep, children, peace and piety, all of which are magnified by possessing a lucky four leaf shamrock. Or a five leaf one for that matter as there is some debate over how many leaves constitute a "lucky" shamrock.

Lucky Shamrock Charm 170

"Shamrock of good omens,

Beneath the bank growing

On which stood the gracious Lugh,

    the many-skilled God.

The seven joys are,

Without evil traces,

On you, peerless one

Of the sunbeams--

    Joy of health,

    Joy of friends,

    Joy of cattle,

    Joy of sheep,

    Joy of sons, and

    Daughters fair,

    Joy of peace,

    Joy of the Gods!

The four leaves of the straight stem, *(alternately five)*

Of the straight stem from the root of the hundred rootlets,

You shamrock of promise,

you are bounty and blessing at all times."

***

    This short charm is rather ambiguous in its meaning. It seems to me to imply both a protective quality to the shamrock and an association with the dead. It may also mean that shamrocks are good to plant on graves.

Shamrock of Power Charm 171

Shamrock of foliage,

Shamrock of power,

Shamrock of foliage,

Which Airmed found under the bank,

Shamrock of my love,

Of most beautiful hue,

I would choose you in death,

To grow on my grave,

    I would choose you in death,

    To grow on my grave

***

These two charms deal with a plant called the Mothan, which may be the bog-violet. It is used for many purposes, including love spells and easing childbirth. For a love spell a woman would pick nine roots of the Mothan and weave them together to form a ring, which would then be given to the girl wanting to make the charm by placing it in her mouth while calling on God. She in turn would place it in her mouth when expecting to meet the target of her spell and if he kissed her would supposedly belong to her ever after. The plant would be placed beneath laboring women to ensure a good delivery, and was sown into clothing for safe travel, and to drink milk from a cow who had eaten the plant conveyed protection from all harm. (Carmichael, 1900)

"The 'mothan' (bog-violet?) is one of the most prized plants in the occult science of the people. It is used in promoting and conserving the happiness of the people, in securing love, in ensuring life, in bringing good, and in warding away evil." (Carmina Gadelica, Volume 2, page 110)

The Mothan Charm 172

I will pluck the gracious 'mothan,'

As the Powers have plucked it before me;

In name of the Godsand of the Spirits everlasting,

    Brighid, and Airmed, and Lugh, before me.

In the field of red conflict,

In which every wrath and fury is quelled,

The cause of all joy and gladness,

    The shield of the gods protecting me.

***

The Mothan Charm 173

I will pluck the 'mothan,'

Plant of the nine joints,

I will pluck and vow myself,

    To noble Brighid and her Fosterling.

I will pluck the 'mothan,'

As ordained by the Powers,

I will pluck and vow myself,

    To great Danu and her children.

I will pluck the 'mothan,'

As ordained of the ancient spirits,

To overcome all oppression,

    And the spell of evil eye.

***

The Passion Flower is an excellent protective charm, especially for travel.

The Passion Flower 175

You beloved passion-flower of virtues,

Sanctified by the blood of Miach,

Son of Dian Cecht, brother of Airmed,

Brother of Airmed, sweet goddess of healing.

There is no earth, no land,

There is no lake, no ocean,

There is no pool, no water,

There is no forest, no steep,

That is not safe for me,

By the protection of the passion-flower of virtues,

    But is to safe for me,

    By the protection of the passion-flower of virtues

***

The Club Moss charm is another protective charm. It wards physical harm from human and faery sources.

The Club Moss 176

The club-moss is on my person,
No harm nor mishap can befall me;
No spirit shall slay me, no arrow shall wound me,
No Fey nor Water-spirit shall tear me.

***

Charms # 178 and 179 are intended to protect against bad luck, especially for livestock. I would recommend them for anyone who has animals; once the catkin wool has been found and the charm said while collecting it I would keep it near the animal being protected.

The Catkin Wool Charm 178

I will pluck the catkin wool,
As Airmed plucked it through her palm,
For luck, for cattle, for milking,
For herds, for increase, for cattle,
Without loss of lamb, without loss of sheep,
Without loss of goat, without loss of mare,

Without loss of cow, without loss of calf,

Without loss of means, without loss of friends,

    From the hearts of the Gods of life,

    And the courses together.

***

The Catkin Charm 179

I will pluck for myself the catkin wool,

The lint the lovely Brighid pulled through her palm,

For success, for cattle, for increase,

For pairing, for uddering, for milking,

For female calves, white bellied.

    This charm is meant to be recited like a chant while churning butter. In this way the energy of the charm is mixed into the butter itself as it is being made, blessing it and everyone who will later eat it.

Charm of the Churn 191

The free will come, come;

The bond will come, come;

The bells will come, come;

The ringing will come, come;

The blade will come, come;

The sharp will come, come;

The hounds will come, come;

The wild will come, come;

The mild will come, come;

The kind will come, come;

The loving will come, come;

The squint will come, come;

He of the yellow cap will come,

That will set the churn a-running.

The free will come,

The bond will come,

The bells will come,

The ringing will come,

The blades will come,

The sharp will come,

The hounds will come,

The wild will come,

The mild will come,

The kind will come,

The loving will come,

The devious will come,

The brim-full of the globe will come,

To set the churn a-running;

And the golden-haired Brighid of the cattle.

A splash is here,

A plash is here,

A plash is here,

A splash is here,

A crash is here,

A squash is here,

A squash is here,

A crash is here,

A big soft snail is here,

The sap of each of the cows is here,

A thing better than honey and spruce,

A bogle yellow and fresh is here.

Come, churn, come;

Come, churn, come;

Come, life; come, breath;

Come, churn, come;

Come, churn, come;

Come, cuckoo; come, jackdaw;

Come, churn, come;

Come, churn, come;

The little lark from the sky will come,

The little woman of the black-cap will come.

Come, churn, come;

Come, churn, come;

The merle will come, the mavis will come,

The music from the bower will come;

Come, churn, come;

Come, churn, come;

Come, wild cat,

To ease your throat;

Come, churn, come;

Come, churn, come.

Come, hound, and quench your thirst;

Come, churn, come;

Come, churn, come;

Come, poor; come, naked;

Come, churn, come;

Come, churn, come;

Come, deserver of alms

Of most distressful moan;

Come, churn, come;

Come, churn, come;

Come, each hungry creature,

And satisfy the thirst of your body.

Come, churn, come;

Come, churn, come;

It is the Gods of the elements who bestowed on us,

power over the charm of a woman with a plant.

Come, churn, come;

Come, churn, come;

Come, fair-white Lady,

And endow my means to me;

Come, churn, come;

Come, churn, come;

Come, beauteous Brighid,

And bless the substance of my cattle.

Come, churn, come;

Come, churn, come;

The churning made of Brighid,
In the fastness of the glen,
To decrease her milk,
To increase her butter;
Butter-milk to wrist,
Butter to elbow;
    Come, churn, come;
    Come, churn, come.

***

This final abundance charm is meant to draw prosperity and decrease poverty. For people who do not churn their own butter I would suggest replacing lines 8 and 9 as well as lines 11 and 12 with the lines "To increase her means/ To decrease her lack" or something similar. When saying for yourself or if you are male change the pronouns accordingly.

A Charm of Abundance 192

The charm sent of the gods,
To the woman who was dwelling
On the floor of the glen,
On the cold high moors--
    On the floor of the glen,
    On the cold high moors.

She put spell to speech,
To increase her butter,
To decrease her milk,

To make plentiful her food--
> To increase her butter,
> To decrease her milk,
> To make plentiful her food

***

Chapter 20: Divination

American Barred Owl. In Celtic myth owls are omens of ill luck. This owl is a wildlife education bird that was rehabilitated after losing 30% of her eyesight. She can never be released to the wild.

Divination was a widespread and complex process among the Gaelic Celts. The Carmina Gadelica mentions several augury and divination charms which can give us insight into some of these practices and methods. In the first example we see a very specific set of actions and timing that must be undertaken to induce a vision, along with the recitation of the charm itself.

From the Carmina Gadelica page 159 *"This divination was made to ascertain the position and condition of the absent and the lost, and was applied to man and beast. The augury was made on the first Monday of the quarter and immediately before sunrise. The augurer, fasting, and with bare feet, bare head, and closed eyes, went to the doorstep and placed a hand on each jamb. Mentally beseeching the God of the unseen to show him his quest and to grant him his augury, the augurer opened his eyes and looked steadfastly straight in front of him. From the nature and position of the objects within his sight, he drew his conclusions."*

Augury Charm 194

Gods over me, Gods under me,
Gods before me, Gods behind me,
I am on your path, O Gods of life,
    and you are in my steps.

The augury Mórríghan made at the battles end,
The offering made of Brighid through her palm,

Did the spirits witness it?--

    The spirits did witness it.

The augury made by Mórríghan about her people,

When the battle ended peace was made,

Knowledge of truth, not knowledge of falsehood,

    That I shall truly see all my quest.

Kindly spirits and Gods of life,

May you give me eyes to see all I seek,

With sight that shall never fail, before me,

    That shall never quench nor dim.

***

Omens

    Omens based on birds and animals are widespread in Celtic belief. The following charms list omens of luck for the coming year relying on hearing or seeing specific animals. If we study this information we can learn details of what animals and what actions by certain animals were seen as bad omens.

Omen 203

Early on a Monday morning,

I heard the bleating of a lamb,

And the kid-like cry of snipe,

While I was gently sitting,

And the grey-blue cuckoo,

And no food yet in my stomach.

On the fair evening of Tuesday,

I saw on the smooth stone,

The snail slimy, pale,

And the ashy wheatear

Near the stream,

The foal of the old mare

Of springing gait, and its back to me.

And I knew from these

That the year would not go well with me.

***

<u>Omen 204</u>

Early on a Monday in the spring,

I saw on the brine

A duck and a white swan

    Swim together.

I heard on Tuesday

The snipe of the seasons,

Bleating on high

    And calling.

On Wednesday I had been

Outside gathering herbs,

And then saw I the three

    Arising.

I knew immediately

That there would not be,

Blessing after that.

The blessings of Brighid calm,

The blessings of Danu mild,

The blessings of the Daghda strong,

Upon me and mine,

    Upon me and mine.

Omen 206

I heard the cuckoo with no food in my stomach,

I heard the stock-dove on the top of the tree,

I heard the sweet singer in the woods beyond,

And I heard the screech of the owl of the night in broad day.

I saw the lamb with his back to me,

I saw the snail on the bare flag-stone,

I saw the foal with his rump to me,

I saw the wheatear on a dyke of holes,

I saw the snipe while sitting bent,

And I foresaw that the year would not

    Go well with me.

***

    This omen deals with swans, birds that are seen as omens of very good luck. The charm is interesting in that it also mentions specific timing not only in the day of the week but also of the day itself. Based on this and similar mentions in previous omen charms it seems clear that dawn was seen as a time that was particularly good for divination.

Omen of the Swans 205

I heard the sweet voice of the swans,

At the parting of night and day,

Calling on the wings of travel,

    Pouring forth their strength on high.

I quickly stood still, I made no move,

And looked to see their flight.

Who was guiding in front?

    The queen of luck, the white swan.

Should you see a swan on Friday,

In the joyous morning dawn,

There shall be increase for your means and your kin,

    And your flocks shall be always flourishing.

***

Conclusion

I believe that there truly is a need for this book. Carmichael's work represents a treasure trove of Celtic material that can and should be used as the foundation of modern Celtic Reconstructionist efforts at shaping liturgy. The prayers and charms contained in this book are my own versions based on the originals from Volume 1 & 2 of the Carmina Gadelica, if the reader has found that these do not suit than I urge you to go to the source and work with the original material for yourselves. Even if you do not want to paganize them as I have done here a working familiarity with the Gadelica is immensely useful in writing your own material as well as in recognizing material from the Gadelica when it is used elsewhere without being credited; something that is becoming an increasingly common problem.

When Alexander Carmichael collected the prayers and charms of the Carmina Gadelica at the turn of the 20th century he was recording the prayers of the common people, truly the songs of the Gaels. We must not let this material die out, just as we must not let the languages of the Gaels die out. Anyone interested in Celtic spirituality – whether it be as a Celtic Reconstructionist, Gaelic Traditionalist, Druid, Neo-pagan, Wiccan, or something else entirely – should see the value of the Carmina Gadelica and seek to incorporate its beauty into your own lives. I originally took on a project to paganize the charms from Volume 2 of the Gadelica for my Druid order, Ord na Darach Gile, the Order of the White Oak. I did so thinking it would be a small, in house project, for use within the Order.

As time went on though I began to understand how truly valuable this material is and also the need for it to be paganized for use by people who, for whatever reason, were not comfortable or able to do so themselves. When I finished the first project I realized I had enough material for a small book and I wanted to publish it to open up its access to anyone who might find it useful. Afterwards I had so many people asking me where Volume 1 was that I decided to take the plunge and paganize that one as well, and after that was done and published this combined edition was the next logical step. It differs from both of the other books in that I have added pictures and my own commentary. I did so at the urging of friends, and in the hopes that these things would deepen the useful feel of the book.

The pictures are not Scottish, or Irish, but rather are of my children and local sacred areas where I live, as well as wild plants. This was a difficult decision for me, as I know people expect picturesque Scottish scenes, but the fact is that the point of this book is to show that these prayers and charms can be modernized and can be used by people anywhere who feel drawn to the spirituality of the Celts. The paganized charms and prayers of the Carmina Gadelica can be an important part of the lives of people who embrace Celtic polytheism regardless of their geography. These pictures reflect that because they reflect my life as an Irish Reconstructionist Druid in America.

References:

Carmichael, A. (1900). Carmina Gadelica Volume 1. As found at
http://www.sacred-texts.com/neu/celt/cg1/index.htm

Carmichael, A. (1900). Carmina Gadelica Volume 2. As found at
http://www.sacred-texts.com/neu/celt/cg2/index.htm

Meyers, K. (1906). The Triads of Ireland. As found at
http://www.archive.org/details/triadsofireland00meyeuoft

These texts are held in the public domain.

All photos are provided by the author and copyrighted. They may not be reproduced without the express written permission of the author.

Appendix A

I'm a big believer in the importance of rites of passage to help anchor us in our spirituality and our sense of self. It's a very tribal way to do things, I think, to commemorate life changes with ritual. I know not everyone agrees or sees the need but for those who do I offer these. These also serve to illustrate exactly how the material offered in the book can be further adapted for specific uses.

A Druid's Baby Blessing Ritual

The child should be dressed in something beautiful and meaningful for the family. If indoors a small altar can be created with a candle (triple wicked if possible) and a bowl of sacred water, as well as something representing a tree. These symbolize the three Celtic realms of land, sea, and sky that form the bedrock of our world and were used to swear oaths in ancient times. If outdoors the altar should be prepared in front of a tree and contain the candle and water. The officiant should walk three times sunwise around the altar holding the infant and chanting:

"Once for Danu, mother of the people of peace,
We go around the path of the sun, beloved one

Once for Lugh, many skilled god,
We go around the path of the sun, beloved one

Once for those who have gone before,
We go around the path of the sun, beloved one

To aid you from the Fairy-kin
To guard you from the Host

To aid you from the Fairy-hound
To shield you from the specter

To keep you under the mantle of the Gods
To shield you, to surround you,

To save you from powers that threaten
To fill you with blessed imbas*

Three times round we go
To wash you in inspiration."

    The child should then be passed (with extreme care!) over the candle flame to the father, back across the flame to the officiant, and then across a third time back to the mother. (If the infant is wearing anything long or flowing I would put the candle on the ground for this part to ensure maximum safety). The officant should then pick up the bowl of water and dipping their fingers in should drip water onto the child's forehead for each line of the following:

"A little wave for your form,
A little wave for your voice,
A little wave for your sweet speech.

A little wave for your means,
A little wave for your generosity,
A little wave for your appetite.

A little wave for your wealth,

A little wave for your life,

A little wave for your health.

Nine little waves for you
By land, sea, and sky
In the names of the Gods of my people
the spirits of the Otherworld,
and the ancestors whose blood lives within you."

The remaining water should be poured out at the roots of a tree, and the gathered family and well-wishers should feast and celebrate,

* imbas is an Old Irish word that means inspiration or knowledge

      This ritual is based off of material from the Carmina Gadelica Volume 3 by Alexander Carmichael, adapted and paganized. The ritual is used by the Druid Order of the White Oak and may be used by anyone or reprinted with proper attribution to the author.

***

Appendix B

Rites of Passage for Adolscents

I divided these up into girl and boy rituals, but there is flexibility in either to be reworked for the other gender, or for teens that identify with the other gender. I fully intend to use the first one, for girls, when my daughters are old enough - unless they'd rather go on a hunt.

This first ritual is a rite of passage for a girl entering adulthood. Personally I would suggest doing it at the onset of menses, or roughly around 12 or 13. It is based on the Invocation of the Graces #3 from the Carmina Gadelica.

Before the ritual the girl should have to face a challenge; this may include solving a riddle, making something by hand that challenges her skill, or finding something hidden. The exact challenge should be tailored to the girl, and should be difficult but not impossible.

Prepare the altar and ritual space as usual; place a bowl of sacred water on the altar. Process to the space and call on the ancestors, spirits of the land, and the gods to witness the ritual. The assembled people should form a rough circle around the altar, while the officiant and girl stand before the altar. The officiant should ask the girl her name, why she has come before the assembly, and if she is ready to assume her new role within the community. The girl should answer honestly and from her heart to all the questions, present proof that she has passed her challenge, and if she is ready to proceed, the officiant should pick up the bowl of water and lightly wash her hands while reciting:

"I wash your palms

In showers of wine,

In the lustral fire,

In the three elements,

In the juice of the rasps,

In the milk of honey."

Then the officiant should drip the sacred water on the girl's head, one drop for each line of the following, as it is recited,

"I place the nine pure choice graces

In your fair fond face,

> The grace of form,

> The grace of voice,

> The grace of fortune,

> The grace of goodness,

> The grace of wisdom,

> The grace of generosity,

> The grace of choice honor,

The grace of whole-souled loveliness,

The grace of goodly speech."

At this point the officiant should put the bowl of water down and stand with their hands on the girl's shoulders while saying:

"Dark is yonder town,

Dark are those therein,

You are the young brown swan,

Going in among them.

Their hearts are under your control,

Their tongues are beneath your foot,

Nor will they ever utter a word

To give offence to you.

You are shade in the heat,

You are shelter in the cold,

You are eyes to the blind,

You are a staff to the traveller,

You are an island at sea,

You are a fortress on land,

You are a well in the desert,

You are health to the ailing.

Yours is the skill of the Fairy Woman,

Yours is the virtue of Brighid the calm,

Yours is the generosity of Danu, ever-flowing,

Yours is the bounty of Boann the fair,

Yours is the beauty of Aine the lovely,

Yours is the tenderness of Airmed, the gentle,

Yours is the courage of Macha the strong,

Yours is the charm of Fand of the wave.

You are the joy of all joyous things,

You are the light of the beam of the sun,

You are the door of the chief of hospitality,

You are the surpassing star of guidance,

You are the step of the deer of the hill,

You are the step of the steed of the plain,

You are the grace of the swan of swimming,

You are the loveliness of all lovely desires.

The best hour of the day be yours,

The best day of the week be yours,

The best week of the year be yours,

The best year in the lifetimes of men be yours.

Dagda has come and Ogma has come,

Brighid has come and Aine has come,

Boann and Manannan Mac Lir have come,

Lugh the many skilled has come,

Angus mac Og the beauty of the young has come,

Morrighan of the augury has come,

Dian Cecht, gifted god of healing has come,

And Miach the skilled healer of the host has come,

And Airmed the mild has come,

And the Spirit of true guidance has come,

And Danu, mother of the people of skill has come,

To bestow on you their affection and their love,

To bestow on you their affection and their love."

Afterwards the girl should thank the gods, spirits, and ancestors and should make offerings to them. The ritual should be concluded in the normal manner and then the assembled people should celebrate with feasting and gift giving to the girl.

This second ritual is a rite of passage for a boy entering adulthood. Personally I would suggest doing it roughly around 12 or 13, but it is up to the parents to decide when the boy is ready. It is based on Blessing the Hunter #114 from the Carmina Gadelica. This prayer was said as a consecration over a hunter before he went out to hunt. A very specific ritual was followed were he was anointed with oil while standing with his feet apart, each foot on a patch of bare ground, then handed a bow (Carmichael, 1900). Much like the blessing of a king or judge this blessing came with specific prohibitions that acted as geis for the hunter throughout his life, usually relating to what animals he could and could not hunt. Specifically nursing or brooding animals were prohibited, as were unweaned or unfledged ones, and resting animals (Carmichael, 1900).

I would recommend that as part of the ritual, if possible, the boy actually participate in a hunt, either literally hunting and killing an animal or else a hunt that relies on skill, perhaps to retrieve a number of hidden items to prove himself. At the start of the ritual he may present the result of his hunt or the items that he found as proof of his success.

Prepare the altar and ritual space as usual; place oil for anointing the boy and a weapon, either real and to be used in the actual hunt or symbolic, on the altar. Process to the space and call on the ancestors, spirits of the land, and the gods to witness the ritual. The assembled people should form a rough circle around the altar, while the officiant and boy stand before the altar. The officiant should ask the boy his name, why he has come before the assembly, and if he is ready to assume his new role within the community. The boy should answer honestly and from his heart to all the questions and present proof of his success at completing his hunt, and if he is ready to proceed, the officiant should pick up the oil and anoint the boy's head while reciting:

"You are the product of your ancestors,

May you be guided in the way that is right,

In the names of the Spirits of land, sea, and sky,

In name of the Gods of Life who bless you.

In the names of Ogma, and Nuada

Manannan of the wave, and Daghda the Good God,

Dian Cecht the healer, and Giobnui the smith

Macha the red, and Danu the mother of the aos sidhe.

In name of Lugh the many-skilled,

And Boann of the river,

Angus beloved, and sovereign Eriu,

Tailtiu calm, and Brighid of the milk and cattle.

In name of Morrighan goddess of hosts,

In name of Anu, giver of abundance,

In name of Flidias of the woodland glens,

And Airmed of the healing herbs."

     The officiant should put down the oil and pick up the weapon, handing it to the boy with proper ceremony. When the boy takes it the officiant should continue, saying,

"Until the time you shall have closed your eyes,

You shall not bend your knee nor move,

You shall not wound the duck that is swimming,

Never shall you harry her or her young.

The white swan of the sweet gurgle,

The speckled dun of the brown tuft,

You shall not cut a feather from their backs,

Till the world ends, on the crest of the wave.

They must be on the wing

Before you place missile to your ear,

And the fair Danu will give you of her love,

And the lovely Brighid will give you of her blessing.

You shall not eat fallen fish nor fallen flesh,

Nor one bird that was not brought down by skill,

Be thankful for the one,

Though nine should be swimming.

The fairy swan of Brighid of flocks,

The fairy duck of Danu of the people of peace."

      Afterwards the boy should thank the gods, spirits, and ancestors and should make offerings to them. The ritual should be concluded in the normal manner and then the assembled people should celebrate with feasting and gift giving to the boy. If an actual hunt was held then at the feast the assembled people can eat what the boy caught.

***

Appendix C

Imbolc – Traditional Celebrations for a Modern Time

This holiday is called many names including Imbolc, Oímealg, Lá Fhéile Bríde, Laa'l Breeshey, and Gwyl Mair Dechrau'r Gwanwyn and was originally celebrated when the ewes first began to lactate. Some older sources mention Imbolc being celebrated on February 13th, although now the date is fixed on February 2nd. This holiday is a celebration of the loosening of winters hold on the land and the first signs of spring's immanent arrival. Three main types of ceremonies could be undertaken - purification with water, blessing with fire, and consecration of talismans or charms. In addition the main ritual theme centered on inviting the goddess Brighid into the home, either in effigy or in the form of a person acting the part.

The fire represents the growing light of the sun. Candles would be lit to celebrate the increased daylight, and often candles were blessed for use in the year to come; this connection to candles offers another alternate name for the holiday, Candlemas. In my personal practice I light special "sun" candles, and bless my candle holders for the year to come.

Ritual washing was done to cleanse and prepare the people for the agricultural work of the coming seasons. Water was blessed and then used to ceremonially wash the head, hands, and feet. Each year when I do this I dip my fingers in the blessed water and run them over the body parts in question, asking that I be cleansed of winter's cold and filled with summer's warmth to work towards a new season. Then I pour the remaining water out onto the earth thanking Brighid for her blessing.

The main charms and talismans of Imbolc are related to Brighid. First there is the Brighid's cross, a woven sun wheel shape which represented the cycle of the year and the four main holy days, according to the book <u>Apple Branch</u>. On Imbolc you can weave new Brighid's crosses, or bless ones you already have, although it may be better to burn the old and weave new each year when possible. A Brighid's cross is protective and healing to have in the home.

A second talisman is the brídeóg, or "little Brighid" a small cloth or straw doll wearing white clothes which is an effigy of the goddess. In some cases the brídeóg would be made from straw saved from the previous Lughnasadh. This doll played a role in ritual after being brought outside, usually carried by the eldest daughter, then invited to enter the home where it was led with all ceremony to a specially prepared little bed. The doll was left in the bed overnight and its presence was believed to bless all those in the household.

Another talisman connected to Imbolc is Brigid's mantle, or an brat Bríd, a length of cloth left out on the window sill over the course of the holy day and night. It is believed that this cloth absorbs the energy of the goddess during the ritual, and can be used for healing and protection throughout the year. This talisman would be kept and recharged every year, attaining full power after seven years.

The ritual for Brighid on Imbolc centers on inviting the goddess in and offering her hospitality. In some cases a woman was chosen to play the part of the goddess, in other cases the brídeóg was used. The door would be opened to her and she would loudly be invited in, shown to her "bed" and offered specially baked bread. Candles would be lit at the windows and next to her "bed", songs would be sung and prayers said calling on Brighid to bless all present in the coming seasons, and grant health and protection to the household. A small broom or white wand would be placed next to the "bed", and the ashes from the fire would be smoothed down in the hopes that the morning would reveal the marks of the wand, or better yet, the footprints of the goddess herself, either of which would be a sign of blessing. Placing the doll in her bed at night would be followed by a large family meal. In Scotland a hundred years ago when entire communities still celebrated Imbolc in the old way a sheaf of corn would be dressed as Brighid and taken from house to house by the young girls. The girls would carry the doll from home to home where the "goddess" would be greeted and offered food and gifts. After visiting each home the girls would return to the house they started from where a party would be held with music, dancing, and feasting until dawn; all the leftover food would be handed out to the poor the next day.

Other rituals involve blessing the forge fires for blacksmiths and Otherworld divinations. In some Scottish mythologies it is believed that Brighid is held by the Cailleach Bhur during the winter months but escapes, or is rescued by her brother Aonghus mac óg, on Imbolc. In others it is said the Cailleach drinks from a hidden spring and transforms into Brighid on this day.

For modern people seeking to celebrate Imbolc in a traditional way there are many options. Rituals can be adapted to feature the brídeóg. If you celebrate in a group you could have one person wait outside with the doll while the other members prepare her bed, and then the group leader could go to the doorway and invite the goddess in. This could even be modified for use in an urban setting with the brídeóg "waiting" out in a hallway or separate room to be invited in. Once invited in the goddess can be offered food and gifts as was done in Scotland and stories about Brighid from mythology could be told. Water can be used for purification, blessing with fire or of candles can be done, as well as making and consecrating the charms associated with Brighid. After ritual the doll could be left in the bed while the group celebrates with a party; to keep the spirit of the way this was done for a modern time all members should bring food to donate to a local food pantry. A solitary celebration could still include inviting the goddess in, placing the brídeóg in her bed, making offerings to her, and a private celebration and food donations.

Imbolc is a powerful holy day with many beautiful traditions. By understanding how this day was celebrated in the past we can find ways to incorporate those methods into modern practice and preserve the traditions that have surrounded Brighid's day for so many generations.

Sources and Further Reading:

Carmichael, A. (1900). Carmina Gadelica. Floris books. ISBN-10 0-86315-520-0

Evert Hopman, E.(1995). A Druid's Herbal of the Sacred Earth Year. Destiny Books ISBN 0-89281-501-9

Kondrariev. K. (1998). The Apple Branch: A Path to Celtic Ritual. Citadel Press ISBN 0-8065-2502-9

McNeill, F. (1959). The Silver Bough, Volume 2. McLellan & Co.

***

Appendix D

Healing Ritual for the Ocean Waters

The ocean is said to be the source of all life, and it is where many people still find sustenance. We get food from the ocean, we find beauty and inspiration in Her majesty, and many people have found healing in Her waters. Yet over and over and over again the ocean's waters are polluted and damaged by human action; last year the waters of the Gulf of Mexico suffered from a long, drawn out oil spill and now the waters off Japan are being contaminated with radiation from the crippled nuclear power plant damaged in the earth quake and tsunami. As many of us have been praying for and sending healing energy to the earth and to the people affected by these disasters, so too some may want to send healing to the ocean's waters and to the life in the ocean that is being affected. This ritual was designed and written last year for the Gulf oil spill, but can be used as well now for this new problem, or at any point for the healing of the ocean. It is meant for use by anyone of any tradition.

Go to a source of running water, if possible, and hold ritual as you normally would. If you can't physically go to any water then decorate your altar with a water theme using whatever most connects you to the ocean. It may be best to invoke a sea or oceanic Deity, or focus on energy that resonates with the ocean. At the centerpoint of the ceremony make an offering to the water symbolic of healing, something safe and biodegradable; if you are inside use a bowl of water to represent the living water and place your offering in there. Say the following prayers:

"O gods of the sea,
put health in the drawing waves,
to enrich the vast ocean,
to liven the dying waters" *

(make your offering)

"I come here in prayer on this day,
Day to send healing on the vast waters,
Day to send health to fish and fowl,
Day to put right the web in the warp.
Day to put life in the briny waters,
Day to place health back in the ocean,
Day to cleanse, day to bless,
Day to put right a great wrong.
Day to put life back in the tide,
Day to send health to the life in the sea,
Day to make a most effective prayer,
Day of power, Gods bless the vast ocean,
Day of power, may the ocean be blessed."

Finish ritual as you normally would. If you were indoors try to take the offerings to a source of water to pour them out so that they can symbolically be given to the ocean, while visualizing the water flowing into rivers, lakes, streams, larger rivers, and eventually the ocean Herself, and your healing energy going where it needs to go.

***

Index

A

abundance, 81, 139, 141, 160
Aine, 29, 177
Airmed, 18, 21, 29, 30, 33, 75, 77, 94, 97, 103, 104, 141, 143, 144, 146, 152, 153, 154, 155, 177, 178, 180
Amergin, 127
ancestors, 22, 26, 27, 33, 45, 47, 49, 64, 84, 173, 174, 178, 179, 181
Angus mac Og, 5, 29, 178
Anu, 33
apple, 72, 123, 124, 183, 186
Augury, 163
Autumn Equinox, 13, 80, 83

B

bansidhe, 17
Beltane, 12, 72, 73
   blessing, 74, 76
birth, 54, 55, 152
blessing, 32, 184, 185
  at death, 57
  baby, 55, 171
  charms, 138, 139
  children, 24
  churning butter, 156
  fairywort, 145
  figwort, 141
  fire, 40, 41
  for Beltane, 72, 74, 76
  for reaping, 82, 83, 84
  herd, 20, 21
  home and family, 51
  Imbolc, 182
  kindling, 41
  meal, 36, 37
  of a boy, 178
  of the home, 52, 53, 62, 66, 70
  of the New Year, 68
  of the ocean, 13
  of the seed, 78
  prayers, 16, 18
  protection, 45
  resting, 45

    the hunt, 31
    the hunter, 33
    to remove evil eye, 134
    young girl, 26
blood in urine, 98, 99
Boann, 12, 29, 33, 177, 180
boat, 13
bog violet. *See* Mothan
Brighid, 11, 12, 18, 21, 22, 28, 29, 33, 34, 46, 55, 69, 70, 71, 72, 75, 77, 84, 90, 91, 93, 94, 95, 96, 100, 114, 117, 120, 129, 134, 135, 139, 140, 143, 144, 153, 156, 157, 159, 163, 166, 176, 177, 180, 181, 182, 183, 184, 185, 186
broken bones, 96
brownie, 17
butter, 69, 70, 156, 160
butterbur, 123, 124
butterwort, 38

C

cairn, 66, 67
cancer, 100
catkin, 155
cattle. *See* livestock
children, 37, 39, 52, 64, 66, 89, 90, 131, 154
    blessing, 24, 52, 69, 73, 76, 77
    healing, 106
    health, 150
    protection, 77
churn, 70, 156, 160
club moss, 155
costume, 63, 67
cramping, 103, 104, 105
cursing, 66, 68

D

Daghda, 12, 15, 20, 22, 33, 38, 59, 75, 77, 143, 166, 180
dandelion, 38, 71
Danu, 6, 7, 18, 20, 22, 23, 28, 30, 33, 34, 35, 38, 46, 59, 74, 75, 76, 77, 83, 89, 90, 91, 109, 129, 134, 148, 149, 154, 166, 171, 176, 178, 180, 181
dawn, 10, 26, 69, 87, 166, 167, 184
dedication, 8, 52
Dian Cecht, 22, 29, 33, 94, 97, 102, 154, 178, 180
divination, 82, 162, 163, 166, 185
duck, 33, 34, 35, 127, 136, 165, 180
dying, 56, 57, 188

E

Eriu, 33, 180
evil eye, 26, 126, 127, 130, 131, 140, 142, 144, 147
   charm for, 132
   counteracting, 129
   cure, 133
   exorcism of, 127
   spell for, 131, 134, 135, 154

F

fairy, 12, 17, 28, 34, 120, 133, 172, 176, 181
fairy wort, 145
Fand, 29, 177
fath fith, 114
fern, 123, 124
figwort, 141, 142, 143, 144
fire, 12, 27, 40, 42, 51, 63, 64, 65, 66, 67, 70, 72, 124, 125, 175, 182, 184, 185
Flidias, 33, 180
flu, 104, 105
flux, 103, 104
for those who would harm me, 136
fox, 68, 114, 120
foxglove, 38, 123, 124
Friday, 75, 77, 78, 167

G

garlic, 38
geis, 178
ghoul, 17
Giobnui, 33, 180
gods, 5, 6, 7, 8, 9, 10, 11, 12, 13, 14, 15, 17, 18, 20, 21, 23, 26, 27, 30, 33, 37, 38, 39,
   41, 42, 45, 46, 47, 48, 49, 51, 52, 55, 64, 65, 66, 67, 68, 69, 73, 74, 76, 77, 79, 81,
   83, 84, 87, 88, 89, 90, 91, 95, 97, 110, 113, 117, 118, 121, 128, 130, 137, 139, 141,
   142, 143, 144, 148, 151, 153, 156, 159, 160, 163, 164, 172, 173, 174, 178, 179, 180,
   181, 188
gossip, 129, 145
guardian spirit, 19
guidance, 8, 13, 15, 29, 30, 177, 178

H

harvest, 80, 82, 84
healing, 92, 93
   breast, 93, 94
   broken bone, 97
   dental issues, 95

digestion issue, 104
  kidney infection, 100
  sprain, 96, 97
  tumors, 100
  urinary issue, 98
Hogmanay, 62, 63, 64, 65, 66, 67
home, 20, 21, 30, 42, 49, 50, 51, 52, 57, 62, 63, 64, 65, 66, 67, 68, 69, 70, 72, 76, 118, 131, 132, 135, 147, 182, 183, 184
house. *See* home
hunting, 26, 32, 33, 34, 114, 174, 178, 179

I

Imbas, 5, 6, 172, 173
Imbolc, 12, 14, 69, 70, 71, 72, 182, 183, 184, 185, 186
indigestion, 103, 104
inspiration, 5, 17, 172, 173, 187
ivy, 140

J

justice, 70, 87, 88

L

lacerations, 96
land, sea, and sky, 7, 13, 14, 18, 21, 26, 33, 34, 76, 78, 93, 100, 171, 173, 179
lasting life, 115, 116, 118, 119
Linnet, 71
livestock, 33, 52, 69, 72, 73, 74, 94, 99, 117, 119, 134, 139, 143, 149, 150, 155, 157, 159, 180
  indigestion, 104
  protection, 118, 120, 155
  strangles, 102
love, 74, 87, 89, 90, 91, 110, 122, 123, 124, 142, 146, 152, 178, 181
Lugh, 20, 22, 23, 29, 33, 38, 59, 74, 83, 90, 91, 117, 134, 151, 153, 171, 177, 180
Lughnasadh, 12, 14, 83, 183

M

Macha, 29, 33, 38, 177, 180
madder, 38
Manannan Mac Lir, 13, 29, 33, 57, 177, 180
marigold, 38
Maunday Thursday, 80
Miach, 29, 97, 102, 143, 154, 178
Midsummer, 14, 81
Monday, 75, 76, 116, 118, 163, 164, 165
moon. *See* New Moon

Morrighan, 5, 20, 29, 33, 75, 76, 77, 78, 178, 180
Mothan, 152, 153

N

New Moon, 58, 59, 60
New Year's. *See* Hogmanay
Nuada, 20, 22, 33, 97, 180

O

ocean. *See* sea
Ogma, 29, 33, 89, 177, 180
omens, 151, 164, 166
Otherworld, 47, 48, 129, 173, 185
Oystercatcher, 71

P

Passion Flower, 154
people of peace, 26, 34, 171, 181
planting, 78
Powers of Life. *See* gods
protection, 8, 11, 12, 16, 17, 19, 20, 22, 23, 26, 42, 46, 47, 50, 51, 69, 77, 111, 112, 115, 117, 120, 153, 154, 183

R

reaping. *See* harvest
red stalk, 140
Ruadan, 12
rune, 62, 80, 112

S

Samhain, 12, 13, 14, 62, 73
Saturday, 75, 77
sea, 7, 12, 13, 14, 18, 19, 28, 35, 49, 73, 75, 76, 77, 79, 80, 81, 90, 91, 95, 98, 100, 114, 116, 117, 124, 128, 129, 131, 135, 141, 142, 143, 146, 147, 149, 171, 176, 187, 188
seed, 78, 79
seven, 38, 60, 64, 101, 106, 112, 136, 140, 150, 184
sewing, 112
shamrock, 150, 151
siren, 17
sleep, 6, 44, 45, 46, 47, 48, 49, 53, 79
smooring, 42
snakes, 71
spirit, 19, 27, 45, 48, 51, 62, 67, 104, 110, 114, 129, 132, 154, 155, 164, 173, 174, 179, 181, 185

Spirit, 21, 30, 33, 46, 49, 74, 78, 153, 178, 179
sprains, 96, 97
Spring Equinox, 14
St. Columba's plant. *See* St John's Wort
St. John's Wort, 147, 148, 150
strangles, 102
success, 35, 86, 89, 100, 119, 140, 156, 179
Summer Solstice. *See* Midsummer
Sunday, 123, 124
sunwise, 62, 66, 67, 78, 82, 171
swan, 28, 29, 33, 87, 88, 116, 118, 127, 176, 177, 180, 181
   healing, 106
   lullaby, 106
   omen, 165, 166, 167

T

Tailtiu, 33, 180
three gods, 38, 98, 133, 148
three realms, 48, 150
three streams, 71, 87, 89
Thursday, 75, 77, 81
toothache, 95
Torranan. *See* Figwort
travel, 20, 21, 23, 47, 64, 77, 88, 152, 154, 167
triads, 7
triskele, 93
troll, 17
truth, 7, 47, 49, 51, 70, 73, 164
Tuesday, 75, 76, 81, 84, 106, 165
tumors, 100

U

urinary issues, 98, 100

V

victory, 26, 89, 108, 145, 149
vomiting, 104

W

weaving, 112
Wednesday, 75, 77, 80, 165
Winter Solstice, 14, 63
withershins, 67
woad, 38

Y

yarrow, 139, 146, 147
yew, 38

Printed in Great Britain
by Amazon